CONSTRUCTION LIGHTING

Solange Sudarskis

7

Masonic wanderings

Construction LIGHTING

CONTENTS

NB. To save the reader wishing to access documentation references on the web, links with simplified keyboard typing have been created with the *tinyurl.com software*
.

1 HIVE, BEE, HONEY

The anthropomorphization of the hive, metaphor of a social body, in this case ecclesiastical, appears in the 16th century **. The clergy of the Church will spread their gospel, pollinating the hearts and minds of the masses, transforming their spirituality is considered a hive.**

The Calvinists did not fail to use this allegory to mock and denounce papal power. As seen on the frontispiece of his pamphlet *The Roman Hive*. The hive obviously has the shape of the pope's triregular tiara as evidenced by the keys of Saint-Pierre, but it is topped here by a very Muslim crescent... It symbolizes the power of the king of bees-pontiff, his Roman palace towards which clerical bees converge.

From the 17th century **, the symbol of the beehive was used in a sense relating to architecture and labor.**
Drawing on the Masonic corpus, craftsmen and embroiderers used historical, social or symbolic elements , different depending on the era and the country. In France, the end of the 18th century saw recourse to the

symbolism of the Temple, the Directory to that of the vogue for Egyptomania (sphinxes, pyramids, etc.), the **Empire to that of bees or the hive.**

The symbol of the beehive which adorned the color of the *Companion Federation of all the Devoirs Réunis* – which represented both the work of the Companions and their place of meeting, around the Mother – was known to the companions through mutual aid associations since the years 1830-1840.

Linked to order and authority in the organization and structure of things, the hive refers to notions of legitimate hierarchy, command, distribution of roles, regulations relating to a community, spirit of collaboration . Each member of a community must carry out their specific activity and play their particular role in accordance with their understanding and real means , their mission and their evolving pace. Indeed, the good of the whole depends on the respect of individuals among themselves and the common goal, based on fraternity and solidarity. Freemasons are bees in the hive they have chosen. The rites/rituals and ceremonies mobilize, channel and direct collective energy, to transfer to the conscious level, the bases on which communities are built, structured and harmonized. " *We could see in the lodge a place of mutual pollination, each word that is exchanged there contributes to a common mellification that silence promotes, and everyone will draw from it their own unique benefit* . "[1]

---

[1] ***Bushy Dictionary of Freemasonry*** , Annick Drogou, Jean-Marc Petillot, Numérilivre.

In the 19th [century] , almost every grand lodge in America officially approved John Sherer's Lodge rugs and recommended that each subordinate lodge purchase one as a teaching aid for the Worshipful Master to instruct applicants. On the Master's, Sherer illustrates the Church (*hive*) supported by the four pillars of the New Testament: Matthew, Mark, Luke and John on *The Master's Carpet* . "The flower under the hive is a dianthus, named by the Greek botanist Theophrastus, meaning "flower of God" . On the left, the beehive is surrounded by cereals and daisies symbolizing St. John the Evangelist. On the right, St. John's Wort representing St. John the Baptist, accompanied by two roses and a rosebud for Mary Magdalene, the Virgin Mary and a child . »[2]

Hive , this is the name given to the lodge which splits to allow the creation of a new lodge in the same obedience, we speak of swarming.

The Bee is a solar symbol. It represents wisdom, immortality and wealth. She is the social bond, dedication, courage unto death, work personified.
In the Middle Ages, we spoke of the " song " of the bee, a truly sacred song since the bee carries within itself a particle of divine Intelligence. Gathered in a swarm or in a hive, these thousands of pieces are linked together to form a single body — the mystical body of Christ — whose head is the king (the queen). The whole is an allegory of the Church which, according to the teaching of Saint Paul, has Christ the King at its head. The

---

[2] < tinyurl.com/tapis-de-maitre >.

community of bees is therefore a symbol of return to unity and reunification.

In Hebrew, the word for bee dvora or Débora (הרובד) has the same root as dabar (דבר), the " word ", which is why the Kabbalists bring the bee and the hive closer to the hive of the Word creator . _ Note that in Hebrew the word desert is written " midbar ", with the same letters daleth beth and reich as roots . With these same roots, Hebrew writes, among others, the words: *dabar* which certainly means speech, but also the plague; *dvora* , the bee and *doberot* , the rafts on which cedar wood was brought from Lebanon to build Solomon's Temple. What do they have in common? It is the movement, the passage from one point to another , the fact of transmitting.

Every living soul is a bee that travels through life and collects pollen of wisdom from life's environments and experiences. " An ancient philosopher once said that the bee extracts honey from the pollen of the flower, while from the same source the spider extracts the poison. The problem we then face is : are we bees or spiders? Do we turn life's experiences into honey, or do we turn them into poison? Many people become embittered by the experience, but the wise man takes the honey and builds it into the hive of his own spiritual nature [3].

According to Champollion, the bee was the symbol of royalty and that of sacred inspiration; honey represented initiation and wise discourses.

---

[3] < tinyurl.com/miel-et-ruche >.

Honey is therefore a symbol of knowledge, knowledge and wisdom . It is the food reserved for the initiate.

Honey is used to illustrate moral teachings. A man is exhorted to eat honey and honeycomb (Proverbs ; 24,13), but warned against excess (Proverbs; 25,16 and 27). It was a comparison for moral meekness (Ezek; 3,3), and for the excellence of the law (Ps; 19,10), of pleasant words (Proverbs; 16,24), and of the lips (Song of canticles; 4.11), and as a figure of love (Song of Songs; 5.1).

This connection between honey and fair and kind words is well illustrated in the **adoption ritual** of the wolf cub (at least 7 years old) reported by Jean Marie Ragon in *Masonic liturgy. Ritual of adoption of young wolf cubs* from 1860 [4]: " He **puts honey** on them **on the lips:** may your mouth utter only friendly words, sweet as honey! May anger and slander never come to sully her with inappropriate and insulting remarks! May your tongue never be used to utter cries of domination or accents of vengeance and contempt against your fellow human beings! Abhor lies ." (p13). It will be noted that it is with wine that the lips of the cub under 3 years old are touched during the **Masonic baptism ritual** with similar exhortations: The Venerable lights the torch of the third candelabra, brings the glass placed on the altar and which **contains wine** , hands it to the godfather, dips his index finger in it, which he then places **on the lips** of the cub and says: "May your mouth never be defiled by lies, but let your lips be opened to loudly proclaim the truth; May your voice resound boldly in the defense of misfortune

---

[4] Jean Marie Ragon , *Masonic Liturgy. Ritual for adopting young cubs* : <tinyurl.com/rituel-adoption>.

and innocence against oppression, may it bring consolation and peace to the hearts of your fellow men and terror to the soul of the wicked [5].

When it is said in the Song of Songs (4.11): *Honey and milk are under the tongue* , this may mean that language conceals and then reveals the infinite sweetness and infinite nutritional value of spiritual thought. Honey and milk being metaphors for the written Torah and the oral Torah. This thought is fully human but also full of G-d when it respects its Discretion and makes its Law nourishment; milk is called *h'eleb* because it comes from the *leb* (heart); it is mixed with honey, born from the comings and goings, from the juice of flowers mixed with the juice of other flowers, by a weaver of sweetness, the bee called in Hebrew *débora* , the one who weaves the *dabar* , the word which irrigates thought towards the heavens of heavens. "From one flower to another, it is , between Heaven and Earth, a transmitter of truths. Through resins and pollens, it collects the stories, the riches, the sufferings, the perfumes of the Earth of which the plant bears the *trace* , thus transforming the hive into a library of nature which it alchemizes into honey .[6]

Honey was the sugar of Greco-Roman Antiquity. Greek tradition has it that Pythagoras fed on it throughout his life. Honey is a heavenly food that has the power to negate mortality, an ambrosia worthy of poets and saints.

---

[5] p.40 of an article by Mangeant in the journal *Le soleil mystique: journal of universal masonry* of 1853: <tinyurl.com/bapteme-maconnique>.
[6] Pierre-Olivier Bannwarth: < tinyurl.com/messager-divin >.

Shortly after Plato's birth, his parents took the baby and placed him on the slopes of Mount Hymettus, abandoning him momentarily while they sacrificed for him to the local gods. Approaching the child who was resting, bees filled his mouth with honeycombs so that it could be rightly said of him: "from his tongue flowed a word sweeter than honey." in reference to Nestor of harmonious language, Nestor, eloquent orator of Pylos, who let words flow from his books as sweet as honey . (Homer, *Iliad song I, verse 249* [7], describing the wisdom of old Nestor who encouraged Agamemnon to peace).

Honey is attributed with preservative powers; this role finds its strongest expression in an embalming technique consisting of wrapping the corpse in honey and wax. Wasn't the mead of the Celts and Greek gods, made from honey, the drink of immortality?

Doesn't honey beg the question " **mi El ?"** » , "who is God?" by phonetic shift towards Hebrew (מי אל) ? **The answer is perhaps, in Hebrew** , in the numerical value of the word "honey", devach (ד ב ש) which is identical (306) to that of the word " fire " , haesh (האש) and to the **word woman** : icha (אִשָּׁה)!

---

[7] Homer, *Iliad song I , verse 249:* <tinyurl.com/Homere-Iliad>.

2 THE METAMORPHOSES OF STONE

If in the 16th ^{century} we used the expression " stone often stirred up by moss is not velée » (in the sense of covering) , we must go back to ancient Rome, to the 2nd ^{century} AD, to find its origin. Lucian of Samosata would have written " *saxum volutum non obducitur musco*" ("the rolled stone is not covered with moss"). I will retain the following meaning from this proverb: perseverance and stability are elements of conservation, while agitation and inconstancy ruin and discredit individuals. Is this not a way of evoking the constant commitment to which Freemasonry encourages us?

In Hebrew, the stone , *Eben* , is a word composed of the letters alef, beth, noun, (א ב ן). Alef is the letter of unity not yet manifested, of value 1, it is therefore what was before the beginning. The letter beth, second letter, symbolizes the abode, the created world. The letter noun symbolizes man. *Eben* , the stone , would mean: transcendence finds your home in the stone to reveal itself to man.

The stones have very different names depending on their shape in the quarry and many others depending on their shape. By "form" we mean the first form that the stone receives when it leaves the quarry to arrive at the site, as well as that which is given to it using the device, depending on the place it must occupy. in the building.

To discover the masonry methods, but especially the different shapes of stones so briefly simplified by the words raw stone, cut stone or cubic so dear to Freemasonry, the list is so long that we will go directly to the remarkable article from volume 9 of *The Encyclopedia of Diderot and D'Alembert* , under the term "Masonry" [8]. As for the word "stones", it is the subject of insurmountable erudition from pages 574 to 603 in the twelfth volume of this same work [9].

Note that in Hebrew the words "monument" and "brick" have the same gematric value 107.

Two major initiatory currents for the perfection of the being are proposed by Freemasonry: chivalrous Freemasonry and the **Freemasonry of builders for which, as one might suspect, the stone constitutes a central symbol** .

Before focusing on the transformations of the mason/stone during its Masonic evolution, let us examine some particular stones not unrelated to construction.

---

[8] 1st [ed] . 1751, p. 809-836: <tinyurl.com/encyclopedie-Diderot-T9>.
[9] < tinyurl.com/encyclopedie-Diderot-T12 >.

Angular stone

Lapis reprobatus caput anguli , it is the rejected stone , mentioned in Psalm 118, taken up by the Gospels and Epistles, which bring it closer to Christ himself: "the stone which the builders had rejected and which became the stone corner".

Among the Ancients, the cornerstones of important buildings were laid with impressive ceremonies. These are well described by Tacitus in the history of the reconstruction of the capital. After detailing the preliminary ceremonies which consisted of a procession of vestal virgins, who with chapels of flowers covered the ground and consecrated it with libations of living water, he adds that after the solemn prayer, Helvidius Priscus, to whom the care to rebuild the Capitol had been entrusted, "laid his hand on the nets which adorned the cornerstone, and also on the cords by which it was to be drawn to its place. At that moment the magistrates, priests, senators, Roman knights, and a number of citizens, all acting with effort and general demonstrations of joy, seized the ropes and dragged the heavy load to its destined place. They then threw ingots of gold and silver, and other metals that had never been melted into the furnace.

The cornerstone has a special and unique shape, which differentiates it from all others. Its use can only be understood by a special category of builders, those who have moved from square to compass, from square to circular form.

It was a stone in a **low position** , a stone which connects the corner of two walls to ensure their cohesion. It is in this sense that the text also evokes it as a foundation.

The New Testament revival goes in the same direction: Christ is the cornerstone on which we can now build a new Temple, this time made of "living stones". The incoming apprentice placed at the head of the northern column, at that corner, participates in the permanent re-foundation of Freemasonry.

The cornerstone becomes a **keystone** at **the _ top of an arc** whose completion it ensures. By its form as well as its position, it is indeed unique in the entire building, and symbolizes the principle on which everything depends. Construction represents manifestation, in which the principle appears only as the ultimate completion. The first stone , or the foundation stone, can be viewed as a reflection of the last stone, which is the true cornerstone.

In architecture, the completion of the work is the cornerstone; in alchemy, it is the philosopher's stone. "Know that it is called stone , not because it resembles a stone, but only because, by virtue of its fixed nature, it resists the action of fire with the same success as any other stone. that she stone. In this case it is gold, purer than the purest; it is fixed and incombustible like a stone, but its appearance is that of a fine powder, impalpable to the touch, sweet to the taste, fragrant to the smell, potentially a most penetrating spirit...for it is a spirit or quintessence. . (Eirenaeus Philalethes, 1664)
The keystone can only be placed from above , thereby representing the stone descended from heaven.
Do not confuse cornerstone and foundation stone.

The Foundation Stone

The apocryphal book of Enoch speaks of the "stone that upholds the corners of the earth."
The foundation stone is strictly speaking a symbol of the higher degrees. It makes its first appearance in the Royal Arch and is, in fact, the most important symbol of this degree. But it is so intimately linked, in its legendary history, to the construction of the Solomonic Temple, that it must be considered part of ancient artisanal masonry.

The Foundation Stone has a legendary history and symbolic meaning of its own that differs from the history and meaning that belongs to other stones. The foundation stone is unique, it is believed to have been a stone placed at one time in the foundations of Solomon's Temple, and then, during the construction of the second temple, transported to the Holy of Holies. It was in the shape of a perfect cube and was inscribed on its upper face, inside a delta or a triangle, the sacred tetragrammaton or ineffable name of God.

Consult Mackey's essential contribution to the word *Stone of foundation* in his Encyclopedia [10].

The Discharge Stone

At the northern entrance to the cathedral of Chartes, the alchemist shakes himself on a discharge stone to leave behind any physical or mental dust. It is often found at

---

[10] Albert G. Mackey, *The Symbolism of Freemasonry* , chap.XXX, *The stone of foundation:* <tinyurl.com/pierre-de-fondation>.

the entrance to places of worship. Wouldn't the opening of the works serve as a mental release [11]stone ?

The flat stone

It is also called "metallic stone".
This is the value of the obolus collected by the widow's trunk expressed in kilos, taking up the original meaning of the *obolus* . The silver half-shekel, which was the basis of the Hebrew obolus, constituted a unit of weight and not yet a coin. It is this idea of weight which is used to value the widow's trunk expressed in kilos.
The Flat Stone cannot under any circumstances be used to cover operating expenses of the Lodge. It is intended for works of solidarity, true walls of the temple of fraternity.

By their symbolism, the rock is found under different names marking stages in the anagogical progress of the mason : raw stone, cubic stone, cubic stone with point, cubic point with sub ascia point [12].

Just as in architecture, the stone is positioned according to its nature and its function, the stone is not cut, nor placed in a strictly isolated approach, but thanks to a framework, an architectural plan in which it is organized transmission and reception; it is this support that makes construction possible. We thus understand why the

---

[11]Video of the Initiatory Paths, the relief stone in the Calberte chapel: <tinyurl.com/chapelle-Calberte>.
[12] See the next chapter *Sub ascia, under the axe.*

lithocentric path as the main metaphor naturally imposed itself on the Freemasonry of builders. Moral philosophy, which results from this, insists, in this goal of elaborating being, on the preponderance of an approach focused on the representations of deprivation, those of emptiness, closely associated with the adaptation of the form of the stone, "to cut your stone" being the most explicit expression. This lapidary parable is didactic in relation to the expression "children of the widow". Through metaphorical iterations using the void, the stone , first a raw and shapeless stone, will be able to become a cubic stone, then a cubic stone with a point to open and reveal a flaming star at the heart of which is the philosopher's stone. . To go from raw stone to cut stone, the intervention of man, his individual will or his desire are imperative. However, such an approach is not spontaneous, it implies being aware of an overall project or a work to be constructed.

Carving a stone is the first work performed by the apprentice during his initiation ceremony.
Let us nevertheless note a paradox: the stones assembled during the construction of Solomon's Temple should not have been cut on site ! This confirms, if necessary, that the work of the 1st [degree] does not take place in the Temple.

Cutting your stone means giving it facets to better reflect light.

The raw stone

The Bible favors raw stone rather than cut stone, it was mainly used to raise altars (Joshua set up an altar of stones which the chisel did not touch, Joshua ; 8,30 and 31). David Lellouche explains it by the fact that "truth had as its symbol the hard stone , and falsity the soft stone that is cut (also dedicated to the god Seth)" [13].

The rough stone , which is considered informal because it does not have regular and mathematical dimensions, becomes, as soon as the worker considers it, the occasion and the place of future work, it is the sign of the unaccomplished.

The concrete block, *perpend esler* , corruption of *perpend ashlar* , is certainly at the origin of the raw stone of speculative Masonry.

Placed at the foot of the altar or at the foot of the loggia panel, on the north side, the rough stone , symbolizing man in the state of nature, is that of the first degree. The apprentice can also see, on the south side, the cubic stone , an ideal towards which he must strive throughout his apprenticeship. Moving from raw stone, shapeless and coarse, to cubic stone, cut and perfect, using construction tools, this seems to constitute the primary goal of the Freemason, called to master his passions and subdue them. by his will. At the beginning, the apprentice is like a shapeless mass, full of disorder and prey to inner chaos. This interior chaos is the original state of the world according to Hesiod, the state of the world before order, before the cosmos, it is both

---

[13] p. 139 to 141 of the work of Frédéric Portal , Egyptian symbols compared to those of the Hebrews , 1840 : <tinyurl.com/symboles-egyptiens-et-hebreux>.

ignorance and infinity, the apeiron of Anaximander , contemporary egoism.

By seeing the cubic stone , (illustration from the cover of Oswald Wirth's book, *Freemasonry made intelligible to its followers*), the initiate understands that he will have to work on himself, to build himself by deconstructing himself from the ego, that he will have to cut his stone. The raw stone contains the potential of this construction. For the REAA, [rough stone is the] crude product of nature, which art must polish and transform. The uncut stones (pebbles, flakes, fragments of marble, etc.), piled up in the construction of the walls, were called *caementum* as opposed to *quadrata saxa* , cut stones [14].

It is indeed about carrying out work on oneself, the realization of the Self, the process of individuation, the unification of the human being. The unity of the stone , writes Carl Gustav Jung, corresponds to the individuation, to the unification of the human being; we would say that the stone is a projection of the unified self. To cut the rough stone is to suppress appearance in order to make itself available to the blossoming of being. The *Swedenborg Ritual of 1870* explains: "The rough stone is the symbol of the fundamental truths which lie at the basis of our moral nature and on which all others will subsequently be based. These are the seeds instilled in the mind of the young child with which, by working on them, the adult man will be built. The raw stone can be polished and cut because the truth can be refined, but it can never be sculpted. Sculpture would break it because truth, just like error, can also be broken, but never

---

[14] *Glossary of Roman Antiquities* written by Georges Goyau , 1896: <tinyurl.com/Antiquites-romaines>.

transformed or falsified. The raw stone or human chaos is subject to the action of the hammer (desire) and the chisel (will). The hammer represents, in fact, the massive unconscious force that the mind must distribute to the points where effort is necessary. The chisel represents the organizing force that the mind must apply.

If the meanings given to the apprentice are already acquired for the companion, alchemy will allow him to glimpse new ways of considering the raw stone.

The raw stone is what the alchemists call the raw material , and they insist on this name to the point of translating it into Latin: *materia prima,* primordial matter, the raw stone is a protolith: "What do you call this body-there? – Raw stone, or chaos, or illiaste, or hylé. – Is it the same raw stone whose symbol characterizes our first grades? – Yes, it is the same one that masons work on roughing up, and from which they seek to remove superfluidities; this rough stone is, so to speak, a portion of this first chaos, or confused mass, but despised by everyone" quotes Osward Wirth in *The Hermetic Symbolism* , taking up *The Blazing Star Catechism or instruction for the grade of Adept or Sublime & unknown philosopher's apprentice* of Baron de Tschoudy.

Once cut in silence (the stones of Solomon's Temple were cut in the quarries before being delivered to the construction site where they were assembled in the absence of metal tools); the Freemason will be able to assemble through his truth with the other stones that are the members of Freemasonry and, beyond that, with all of humanity.

The rough stone is placed on the apprentice's side to the north. **Let us not forget that the rough stone is called a "capable block", which indicates that the recruitment of a "rough stone" in FM must verify the potentialities of the Freemason candidate.** We call "dead" a cut stone which, damaged or of the wrong size, has proven to be unsuitable for the intended use.

The Cubic Stone

It is the regular hexahedron, the masterpiece that the apprentice must create. It is necessarily the simplest form, therefore the most harmonious: it is the one in which all the elements are equal to each other and similarly arranged. It is the cube, the basic element of all architecture, the first form of sacred stones .

Like the size of the rough stone , the cubic stone is closely linked to the symbolism of Tools and particularly to that of the square, chisel and ruler. In the box, she is on the steps of the altar of oaths, on the south column side. The cubic stone is both a form of cut stone and a geometric figure, the cube, which allows numerological speculations (Jules Boucher) and analogical comments of a moral nature (Ragon). For the latter, the cubic stone symbolizes the progress that the companions must make: the most perfect solid, it is "the cornerstone of the immaterial Temple elevated to philosophy and the emblem of the soul aspiring to ascend to its source".

In his theosophical manuscripts of the 18th [century], Brother François-Nicolas Noël shows how two-dimensional plane geometry reveals the three dimensions (length, width, thickness), used according to a symbolic approach, which make it possible to overcome the discontinuities of the world apparent, profane, and to go, for example, from the circle to the square, by joining contact points of interlocking circles to give the shape of the [double] cubic stone. Or more simply, going from the hexagon to the diamond (the rhombus) and the cubic stone [15].

In the RER the four upper angles of the cubic stone represent the universality of the Order and the four parts of the world in which it is spread, the four lower angles, the four virtues which are the basis of the Order.
Having become a cubic stone , the companion offers itself to all intellectual and spiritual exhibitions, each of its faces being able to represent the 6 orientations of the universe, East, West, North, South, Zenith and Nadir. The cubic stone is a form of being to assemble with other stones that are not only Freemasons but all men and women.
Each face, each angle, each edge is identical to the others, like men in fraternity.

There are always 3 hidden sides when looking at a cubic stone. It is with the lever that the mason can make the one below appear.

Unfolding the cubic stone opens onto the *cross* .

The pointed cubic stone

The pointed cubic stone is only found in the ancient and accepted Scottish Rite and the French Rite. Traditional

---

[15] François-Nicolas Noël, *Theosophical Manuscripts* : <tinyurl.com/manuscrits-theosophiques>.

French Rite 1783, 1786 and Regulator 1801. Most of the other rites, the Anglo-Saxon rites, the Groussier French Rite among others, ignore it completely.

Cut stone is human work, cubic it is feminine, conical it is masculine. The pointed cubic stone attests to the alliance between the dynamic and the static.

The pointed cubic stone is presented in footnote 66 of the *Precious Recueil de la Maçonnerie Adonhiramite, containing the catechisms* ... of Louis Guillemain de Saint-Victor in 1789 as a symbol of knowledge and morality: "the same philosophers who compared the apprentice to a rough stone, then compared the companion to a cubic stone in a pyramid, so that it contained all the sacred numbers ; that is to say, unit, five, four, three times three, and therefore nine: moreover to cut this stone it is necessary to use the compass, the square, the level, the line of - lead; and as all these instruments are the symbols of the sciences and the virtues, and as these were the means that these philosophers used to make what we call a Companion, they could therefore without error make this moral comparison. "Tools mean nothing other than care and desire [16]."

Inside its volume, the cubic stone contains the pyramidion which allows it to become a pointed cubic stone . The shape of each face is inscribed in a pentagon which is missing a fifth tetrahedron. This void allows the pyramidion to hide in the cubic stone . The

---

[16] Louis Guillemain de Saint-Victor, *Precious Collection of Adonhiramite Masonry, containing the catechisms* ... <tinyurl.com/Masonry-Adonhiramite>.

pyramidion is extracted from the interior of the cubic stone; the interior emptiness thus brought about becomes full when what is below is like what is above. The lever can be used to extract the pyramidion from the inside of the cubic stone . It is within matter that we are connected to the universe. Through a reversal the mason brings about a change of being by choosing to continue in materiality or to rise towards spirituality. "Like a raw and unfinished block, man is extracted from the quarry and, thanks to the secret cultivation of the mysteries, is transformed into a true and perfect pyramidal crown."

18th century lodge paintings clearly show that any initiatory route corresponds to the transformation of raw stone into cubic pointed stone. This image of the ascent towards transcendence also corresponds to the search for the philosopher's stone .

For René Guénon, the transformation of "raw stone" into "cubic stone" represents the elaboration that ordinary individuality must undergo in order to become capable of serving as a "support" or "base" for initiatory realization; the "pointed cubic stone" represents the effective addition to this individuality of a principle of supra-individual order, constituting the initiatory realization itself, which can moreover be considered in an analogous way and consequently be represented by the same symbol at its different degrees, these being always obtained by operations corresponding to each other, although at different levels, like the "white work" and the "red work" of the alchemists [17].

---

[17] René Guénon, footnote 191, *La Grande Triade* : <tinyurl.com/La-Grande-Triade>.

This interpretation could also consider that the pyramidion is added to the cubic stone to represent the fact that not only must one cut one's stone but that one must also add to it through work, listening to others, which completes our be for its improvement.

The top of the pointed cubic stone is comparable to an omphalos, a visible and concrete representation of the center of the world, of an opening onto the divine, quintessence of being, meeting point of the manifested and the unmanifested like a *axis mundi* . The concept of the cosmic mountain specifically expresses this idea of omphalos, the theme of centrality which is very characteristic of Mount Zion. What is important is always central. This is what medieval world maps expressed visually by equating Jerusalem with the center of the world

The extraction of the material part gives way to contact with the world of the spirit. In other words, having found the center of his being, the initiate raises this center towards transcendence to make it emerge from the cubic stone.

The inverted point, inside, of the pyramidion, indicates the center of the stone . The Freemason works in the center leaving the heaviness and rumors of life on the periphery. One of the builders' secrets would be to grind the stone to try to make it into a "diamond", until finding the center. This center which, under another formulation and by simple antimetabole of the coded language of the alchemists is what the symbolism calls "the Hidden Stone" of VITRIOL, indicating that in reality the quest consists of searching for what is hidden in the stone.

Jean-Marie Ragon in his *Philosophical and Interpretive Course of All Ancient and Modern Initiations* of 1841 writes: "It is only in the French rite that there is more ample discussion of the cubic [pointed] stone, one of whose faces presents , in a division of eighty-one boxes, the words of the first five grades; and the capital, composed of sixteen triangular boxes, together forming a large triangle, or delta, emblem of the Divinity, contains the sacred word of the present grade. It presents under the numbers 3, 5, 7, 9, 42, consecrated in all religions and under the geometric figures triangle, circle, square, which the initiates of Memphis are fond of, the attributes of supreme intelligence, the great divisions and the operations of nature, the principles of the sciences, the arts and natural religion.

In 1863, *The Golden Branch of Eleusis was published,* written by Étienne Marconis de Négre, who also gave explanations to this stone - referred to in the angular text -, considering it essential in Freemasonry and one of whose faces is a masterpiece [18].

At the 13th degree of the AASR, this cubic stone is discovered by Guibulum, Stolkin and Johaben, the Knights of Royale Arche, in a secret vault, in the middle of a pedestal, and "covered with an agate stone cut into the shape quadrangular, on which the word substituted was engraved on the upper face, on the lower face all the secret words of Masonry and on the four faces the cubic combinations of its numbers, which caused it to be called cubic stone. This is what Brother Chéreau reports in his

---

[18] Étienne Marconis de Négre, *The golden branch* : <tinyurl.com/RameauDorDEleusis>.

text Explanation of the philosophical cross and the Cubic Stone [19].

For the Egyptians, the pyramid constituted the staircase allowing the deceased pharaoh to rise to the god Re, to join the Principle. The material pyramid was to be completed by an invisible spiritual pyramid, an extension of the four edges towards the sky, and also by an underground pyramid linking it to the Earth and forming with the first the manifestation of the octahedron.

What if all this was just speculation ?

Jean-Michel Mathonière, essayist and historian of the companionship and more particularly specialist in Compagnons stonecutters, offers us a completely different approach. "Perspective is omnipresent in the treatises of the first half of the 17th century, and we know how much it has a symbolic dimension. The same goes for everything that concerns the projection of shadows by light, whether it concerns the staging of architecture or gnomonics. This is how, for him, the cubic stone with a point is virtual and would only be the projection of the cubic stone on the raw stone (that which is to be cut) in the art of stereotomy. It is from the Treatise of Abraham Bosse (1647), where we see key figures in the theory of ocular perspective, that the pointed cubic stone, symbol of this distorted secret in Freemasonry, would have originated.

In fact, the pointed cubic stone, which adorns the Lodge Table at the Traditional French Rite and at the REAA, is not a stone, explains Jean-Michel Mathonière! This is a

---

19Cubic stone of the 13th degree: <academia.edu/8833872>.

mistake among speculatives. The discoveries that have been made show a simple projection of shadows that we find in the Perspective Treatises of the 16th century and 17th ^{centuries}. It is therefore not a question of a solid volume, but of edges. It is the projection of light (divine in this case) from an octahedron (air) which gives a cubic stone with a point! This projection of light was considered by the operatives to be divine, just like the "divine projection" which traces a perpendicular from the point of the stone to its base, except that the operatives ended their line at the center of the stone using of a star. The speculatives have taken up this perpendicular without knowing its true meaning, because the end of this perpendicular at the center of the stone is a vanishing point!

This divine perpendicular is, in fact, a feature of perspective that we will find represented in treatises on perspective from the middle of the 17th century, notably that of Vignole, but also in *Le livre de l'Architecture* by Philibert de l'Orme and in treatises on perspectives and stereotomy, such as those of Abraham Bosse (plate 3 in *Manière Universelle de Mr Desargues, pour practice la perspective par petit-pied like the geometral,* 1648) or of Giraud Desargues. Further proof that this pointed cubic stone is not a volume, but a series of vanishing points (on the ground, projection of shadows) [20].

If we carefully consider the shape of a cubic stone both in plan and in its volume, that is to say by a perspective drawing, we realize that, by the shadow it creates, the light, makes the pointed cubic stone appear.

---

[20] Video Jean-Michel Mathonière: <tinyurl.com/conference-Mathoniere>.

However, a question arises: **must the stone necessarily be cut in order to make it suitable for the use for which it is intended? Is** the raw stone not capable, in its singularity, its roughness and its opacity, of finding a place in the building, if only by bringing it together with the other stones? Should we necessarily give it another aspect , make it homogeneous, standardize it to insert it into the collective design of the construction of the temple of humanity ? In doing so, do we not risk taking away what makes it beautiful or original?

The answer: **what if it was not a question of cutting YOUR stone to transform yourself but of moving from the work of discovering the raw stone to working on the cubic stone? It is to make the cubic stone already within oneself grow to fill the "blobs of the ego" with the consistency of being fraternal and spiritual.**

If cutting **a** stone is a subtraction, cutting **one's** stone would be a replacement in itself of what one gives up to welcome the enlargement of a more awakened and more spiritual consciousness until its form replaces the raw stone. A human being is a treasure buried in a cage of historical prejudices, marked by his family, society, his culture, his history. This is why it is appropriate to think that the one who cuts his stone is neither in renunciation nor in abnegation of what he is. He is in the conversion of his being, thus achieving the discovery of what is hidden within him to resonate, in his consciousness, the echo of the unity of spirit and matter. As in Jung's thought , it is a question of integrating one's polarities in spiritual growth by an energy which pushes towards this filling of form and which one can call love [21]. Then, illuminated by love, the cubic stone becomes a pointed cubic stone.

"You must become the man you are. Do what only you can do. Constantly become who you are, be the master and sculptor of yourself," Friedrich Wilhelm Nietzsche could have written (*Ecce Homo* , 1888, the subtitle of which is: "How one becomes what one is" (wie man is, was man ist).

---

[21]Video, Eric De Lucca: <tinyurl.com/la-chute-comme-experience>.

3 SUB ASCIA, UNDER THE AXE.

From 1740-1750, on French Lodge Tables, the pointed cubic stone **is placed, *sub ascia* to indicate its sacred character.**

The ascia has sometimes been compared to the Egyptian adze. It is called adze when the handle is long and ascia when the handle is short. The *Gaffiot Dictionary* gives the translation of "adze", "trowel", or "stonecutter's hammer [22]".

The Romans gave the name ascia *to* an instrument whose iron can act on a plane parallel to that in which the worker is located (the ax slices in a perpendicular plane). We find this symbol, as well as the inscription *sub ascia*, engraved on ancient tombs, particularly around Lyon [23].

This has given rise to many interpretations. We note that the ascia could be considered as a symbol (in fact a cross, *crux dissimulata*) used to mark graves by Christians at the time of persecution as mentioned by Mr. Sansas in his

---

[22] < tinyurl.com/gaffiot-ascia >.

[23] Couchoud Paul-Louis, Audin Amable. *Requiem aeternam... The ascia, instrument and symbol of burial. In: Revue de l'histoire des religions* , volume 142, n°1, 1952. p. 36-66: <tinyurl.com/symbole-ascia>.

communication, *Symbolism of the ascia* , retained by the *Acts of the Imperial Academy of Bordeaux* of 1866 [24].

It is therefore an essentially Christian allegory which can mean: "reform your morals, remove your vices, thus become new men, pure from all pollution like the wood and stone polished by the ascia". The moral analogy with the **cubic stone with a** *sub ascia point* for the Freemason of the 18th century . is undeniable. Thus, one could say that the cubic stone is consecrated by ascia, *sub ascia dedicavit*, by the Christian faith.

A bretted hammer, *Broked mall* , which we read in the *Chetwode Crawley Manuscript* , is said to be the origin of the ax-like instrument which appears on French lodge paintings of the 18th century , alongside the cubic stone pointed; it could also be the corruption of *broached urnall* , a word which would designate the cubic pointed stone itself.

For Jules Boucher, the stone is under the Ax to indicate its sacred character. The Pyramid protects it from Water, as the Ax protects it from Fire or Lightning, hence a moral symbolism. The stone must be defended against Water (dissolving forces) and Fire (overly sublimating forces).

For Irène Mainguy, the Ax at the top of the pyramidion, similar to lightning, would bring spirit out of matter. This Ax penetrating the top of the stone would indicate that the stone has reached the finish of beauty and perfection. This would mean that the Stone, after having been rid of

---

[24]From p. 409: <tinyurl.com/symbolisme-ascia>.

its rough edges by the Chisel and the Mallet, would represent the completion of the work when it is surmounted by the four faces of the pyramidion, the connecting axis between the terrestrial and the celestial.

For Guénon, the ax here is nothing other than the hieroglyph of the Hebrew letter qoph (ק). The general meaning attached to the Hebrew letter qoph, or the Arabic letter qâf, is that of "strength" or "power" (in Arabic qowah), which can be of a material or spiritual nature.

This stone represents the Masonic ideal which must constantly be defended against water and fire [like the antidiluvian columns discovered by Pythagoras and Hermes]; the first representing the dissolving forces, the second the overly sublimating forces." The Mason must stand in a happy medium with safety and rectitude.

Justifying that this stone is one of the immobile jewels, Jules Boucher explains its propaedeutic value to us: "The stone placed under the ax to indicate its sacred character, remains cubic although surmounted by a pyramid which protects it from water, like the ax protects it from fire (lightning). For the adept, the meaning of this symbol is the same as that of the sword, dagger or hammer; these white weapons designating the silver tears of white salt (small drops) which chop the material.

Rabi Zied Odnil (François Lindo-Diez) tells us that the ax is placed on the pyramidion to invite us to split the top of the cubic stone with a point (Oswald Wirth wrote : the cubic stone cut by an ax, ... undoubtedly indicates that 'we must open the Stone, split it in order to arrive at its content, its esotericism). The blazing star appears in the gaps of the upturned tetrahedra; it is the void, the invisible which shows the form. It is the successive voids, the invisible questioned, which have shown that the blazing star is in gestation in the raw stone. At its heart is the philosopher's stone .

The language of birds allows us to remember, for the axe, the "H" which is the spirit of the alchemists. The alchemist Patrick Burensteinas and Georges Combes show this masterfully in their films *The Alchemical Journey* , of which here is the extract where the 5-pointed star appears [25].

The Masonic acacia may well not be such a tree as is often mentioned. This could be the ascia *deformity* . As it would have been used to cut funerary steles, *asciare* would have the primary meaning: to dedicate the tomb by flattening the funerary block with ascia. Its second, symbolic meaning could be "to seal a tomb under the ascia to give it an inviolable character". So the distorted word acacia would be a tool with a symbolic dimension, swapped in Prichard's *Manuscript Masonery Dissected* (1730) by "cassia" [26].

It is said, about Athena (Pallas), emerging from the brain of Zeus (Jupiter) cut off by Hephaestus (Vulcan), that she represents the goddess who presides over wisdom and she is rightly said to be born from the brain where is the seat of wisdom.

---

[25] Video, Patrick Burensteinas: <tinyurl.com/etoile-aléglise >.
[26] This subject is developed in the Collection Booklet: *Lights towards the middle chamber* of the *Masonic Vagabondages Collection.*

4 THE IRON BAN

A tradition based on religious beliefs ensured that the Tiber only wanted to support one bridge, the Sublicius bridge; It was still necessary to avoid using iron, a metal which was considered to desecrate sacred places. When it was repaired, or when it was refurbished, all kinds of sacrifices had to be made on both banks and on the bridge itself. They were presided over by the pontiffs, who even took their name from it [27].

In his Masonic instructions, Pastor Anderson takes up the text of I Kings; 6, 7 where it is said that when they built the house (Solomon's Temple), they used ready-made stones and neither hammer, nor ax, nor any iron instrument was heard in the house while we were building it.

Likewise it is written in Exodus; 20,21 : "However, if you build me an altar of stones, do not build it of hewn stones; for, by touching them with iron, you have made them profane."

---

[27] Revue des traditions populaire, 1891, p.129: <tinyurl.com/rites-de-construction>.

This prohibition is described by Maimonides in the *Laws of the House of Chosen* : the slabs of the Heikhal and the Azarah which have become scratched - or chipped - are unfit for Worship: they cannot be reassigned to profane use and must be buried . They are unclean as it is said "because you have placed your sword on it and you have profaned it". It was a very strict law to the point that anyone who used a stone worked with iron for the construction of the Altar or the Ramp was liable to flogging. The precautions were such that when the Altar was plastered twice a year, in the run-up to Passover and Sukkot, it was smoothed with cloth and not with a metal trowel, lest it erode. a stone and make it unusable [28].

However, this metallurgical dimension is confirmed by the overabundance of metals in the construction of the Temple of Jerusalem, gold in particular, and in the person of Hiram who was a foundryman [29].

Rabbis Rashi and Nachmanides, for their part, explain: the tool forged in iron is a symbol of destruction, while the altar prolongs life.

The altar is a symbol of reconciliation between God and man, but the iron tool is a symbol of disunity and separation.

In Hebrew, iron, **barz** e 1 (ברזל), is the acrostic of the names of Jacob's wives (Bila, Rachel, Zilpah and Leah) who gave birth to the twelve tribes of **Israel** . Because

---

28Chapter 1, *The Temple, History, its perfection* , Verse 16: <tinyurl.com/Maimonides-lois>.

[29]The tribe of Naphtali from which he comes is that of the blacksmiths (1K ;7,14). "His father was a Tyrian, a copper worker; he himself was full of talent and industry, skilled in all copper work. He went to King Solomon and executed all his [metal] works .

they were born from 4 different and opposing mothers (mistresses and servants), Jacob's twelve sons will only experience fraternal unity when equality between their genitor mothers is established. Unity between the 12 tribes of Israel, an essential condition for the advent of Mashia'h, explains why it will be authorized, in the third and final Temple, to use a material hitherto prohibited.

English instructions from the 18th [century] give one reason for this: it was the best way to show the ingenuity of masonry at that time, for these materials were prepared at such a great distance that, when assembled, they fitted so perfectly that one would have said the work of the Great Architect of the Universe rather than that of a mortal.

At the end of the 18th [century], the instructions propose another interpretation: so that the Temple is not defiled there is this prohibition which refers to Exodus ;20,22 to 25 and Joshua;8,30,31. Scottish rituals have preserved this version. Because the Philistines, after the invasion of Judea, had assumed a monopoly on iron, preventing the Hebrews from manufacturing metallic weapons, out of hatred, the latter considered the working of iron as equivalent to the manufacture of a idol and passing an iron tool over a sacred object was tantamount to defiling it.

Masonic rituals take up the ban on iron with the expression "leave metals at the door of the Temple" [30].

---

[30] *The Graham Manuscript* already mentioned this ban on iron. Note 19: <tinyurl.com/interdiction-du-fer >.

At the time of initiation, the layman is effectively separated from any metal object he may have had on him. The allegory undoubtedly takes up the previous propositions by developing them to the point of explaining that metals are everything which can, in the name of tolerance, divide, violate, offend the consciences of the brothers (and sisters) gathered in a lodge. The confidence placed in the new initiate to dominate this violence is marked by the fact that his metals are returned to him at the end of the initiation ceremony. Esotericists consider that the presence of metal on the impetrant "hinders the circulation of currents [vibrations] so that the "magical" act of initiation is accomplished by the meeting of forces, one passive emanating from the material, the other active [and spiritual] dispensed by the Venerable through the intermediary of his flaming sword [31].

So what would you say to me about carrying a sword?

In the oldest French Masonic disclosures, printed from 1744, it was explicitly specified that, in the ideal framework of the Lodge, and for the time of its Outfits, all Brothers became equal and equality was chosen " by the top". All the Brothers being deemed gentlemen, all were called to bear the sword, whether they were nobles or not "outside". Everyone was announced in the 18th century . "gentleman" (which is worth two degrees of

---

[31]Video, Jean-Jacques Gabut, *The initiatory paths* : <tinyurl.com/depuoillement-des-metaux>.

nobility) except servants announced as "private" [32]. This is why, in the lodge, the bourgeois could, from then on, carry the sword (reserved for the nobles) and did not deprive themselves of it.

However, it then became difficult to take the initiation test with a sword at your side, at the risk of seeing a flaming candlestick jostled by the sword of the candidate blinded by the blindfold. We have known about the English's fear of fire since the great fire of the City of London in 1666. It would be for this reason that the symbolism of "leaving metals at the door of the temple" would have been invented, justifying the deprivation of sword, among others.

Masonic engravings from the 18th century are also eloquent on this subject, showing that the sword was not worn at first degree initiations but kept at other degrees [33].

So, shouldn't we consider that the expression "leave the metals at the door of the Temple" would only concern the initiation ceremony?

Hence not to be confused with the expression "abandon the old man"!

---

[32] Attributed to Gabanon, *New catechism of the Freemasons containing…* , dated 1440 since the Flood, with approval & Privilege of King Solomon, p. 46: <tinyurl.com/noblesse-du-franc-macon>.

[33] Engravings by Thomas Palser: <tinyurl.com/gravure-initiation>.

5 FROM TEMPLES TO TEMPLE, FROM TEMPLE TO MASONIC TEMPLES

Templum meant the sector of the sky observed by the augury which thus delimited a well-defined surface. Then the word designated the place (or building) from which observation of the sky was carried out.

The words "temple" and "time" both have the same Indo-European etymology *tem* (Greek τεμνω) which means to cut. Time is in fact a cut (a space) in duration; the temple was in ancient Western societies, a cut (natural or worked clearing) in the forest, where sacred rituals were held; this cup corresponded to a division demarcated using a stick or scepter; a way of separating a space and a moment from the natural world, through a process of sacralization. The word temple derives, more probably, from the Sanskrit root *temp* (extent, space) which gave the Latin *templum,* a confined space normally drawn in space by the staff of the *augur* or *aruspice* , a priest who interprets the omens (represented by natural phenomena such as the flight of birds, the reading of the organs of sacrificed animals, etc.) and predicted the future. Hence the Latin term contemplor (*to* contemplate), to look at the sky, possibly looking for omens. It is therefore a volume of open space between sky and earth, hence one of the reasons which explains why the ceiling of the Masonic temple is starry.

The temple is therefore understood here in the broadest sense as the center of the world, distributing space between the spheres of the sacred and the profane, and as a construction depicting man's initiatory journey. But a privileged place is given to the Temple of Solomon, archetype of the sacred place taken up as a model throughout Judeo-Christian civilization, and whose symbolism is still used by Freemasonry today.

The temple can be considered from several angles, it is to be appreciated as:

Secret location. The Egyptian temple, surrounded by an enclosure which prohibits access to the building to the layman, is not comparable to a church where the public and the faithful are freely admitted. The temple houses the creative power that organizes the worlds. Such energy can only be approached by specialists with Pharaoh at their head. This is why the structure of the temple is an axis which starts from the outside, from the apparent light, to reach the heart of the sanctuary, the seat of the secret light, that of the divine. Divine power is not only confined to Heaven or the beyond. Its presence is also manifested on Earth among humans. Temples , for the gods, and necropolises, for the ancestors, are places where priests exercise their roles as mediators between humankind and the forces of the invisible. These are separate places, kept away from the majority of the living, their access being subject to restrictions of all kinds such as bodily purity, fasting, the obligation of silence.

Holy place. In ancient Greece, any place could take on a sacred character provided that a god appeared there or a hero died there. The Greek term for sacred space, *temenos* , applies as well to a modest altar, a simple mound of earth or sacred space placed near a river or in the heart of a wood, as to the vast building surrounded by a colonnade erected in honor of one of the great gods of Olympus. Originally, the temple is simply the space in the sky demarcated by omens to observe the flight of birds. Subsequently it became the building itself, from which, according to strict rules, this observation was carried out. Closed to the population, it houses the statue of the divinity and its treasure.

Central location. The Temple of Solomon, built in the 1st millennium BC, probably formed a series of communicating courtyards inspired by the architectural formulas of Syrian temples. The Holy of Holies, the central sanctuary was so sacred that only the high priest could enter it. There was the Ark of the Covenant, containing the tables of law given to Moses by the God of the Hebrews. After its destruction, it remains a centrality for Judaism, with believers turning to it for their prayers. Muslims consider it one of their high places of pilgrimage.

Celestial observatory. It seems obvious that certain megalithic sites were both temples and astronomical observatories. This is the case of the Stonehenge megalith circle in England. This solar and lunar temple was probably dedicated to the cosmos.

Replica of the cosmos. Egyptian sacred texts explain that the temple is the image of the cosmos: by entering the naos, the pharaoh passes through the "gates of heaven". The very old conception of the temple as the *imago mundi* , the idea that the sanctuary reproduces the universe in its essence, was transmitted to the sacred architecture of Christian Europe: the basilica of the first centuries of our era, like the cathedral of the Middle Ages, symbolically reproduces the earthly Jerusalem.

The Masonic temple can be seen as a syncretism of all these aspects , at once sacred, central, cosmic and spiritual, to which is added the idea that the temple is when the Freemasons are gathered together (this is not not the place that honors the man, it is the man that honors the temple). The temple is the realization and the figure of the hierarchical reign of truth and reason on earth [34].

In the rites of Freemasonry, inspired by the builders of the Temple of Solomon, the temple very clearly adopts a cosmic dimension; its vault is studded with stars, the moon and sun are present there, the references to the cardinal points order the space of the temple, the circulations take place in relation to the movement of the planets. The initiatory space, that is to say the place where the rites are performed, is in classic opposition to the village, a social place, a cultural place, inhabited by humans. The mythical construction of Freemasonry is a cosmogony and this not only because the sanctuary represents the world and its celestial archetype, but also because the temple allows one to experience the various temporal cycles expressed by the rites.

---

[34] Georges Roux, *The true temple of Apollo at Delos* : <tinyurl.com/temple-de-Delos>.

Note that the Temple of Jerusalem was not built to be visited by men like a church, a synagogue or a mosque. It is literally the House of G-d, a place for Him alone [35].

The Temples of Jerusalem

When the Temple was built in Jerusalem, it was only one sacred place among many others, it was not the only place of veneration for YHVH Elohim. The high places were all considered legitimate in cultic terms until the reform of Josiah in 621. The multiplicity of sanctuaries was also expressly authorized by the word of God which even prescribed the manner of building an altar [36]. There are many texts in the Bible that illustrate such practices [37]. Hadn't Jacob built an altar in Shechem (Gen. 33,20) and raised a standing stone at Bethel? (Gen;28,18 and

---

[35] Consult the article by Gérard Foy, *A history of the Temple, in issue 4 of 2021 of the Revue L'Initiation* , p.2: <tinyurl.com/linitiation-2021-4>.

[36] Exodus (20:21): If, however, you build me an altar of stones, do not build it of hewn stones; for by touching them with iron you have made them profane. Ibidem (20:22) Neither must you ascend my altar by steps, so that your nakedness is not revealed there.

[37] Joshua on Mount Ebal (Josh 8:30-32), Gideon at Ophrah (Judge 6:11,24), Manoah at Zoreah (Judge 13:15,20), Micah on Mount Ephraim (Judge 17:5)), Samuel in Mizpah (1Sa 7:9ff.) Samuel in Ramah (1Sa 9:12-18 7:17), the Hebrews in Gilgal (1Sa 11:15), Samuel in Bethlehem (1Sa 16:5), David on the threshing floor of Araunah (2Sa 24:25), Solomon at Gibeon (1Ki 3:4), Elijah on Carmel (1Ki 18:30ff).

35,14), and it was in the same place, in Shechem, that Joshua had raised a large stone under a tree! [38].

Jerusalem was not chosen at random. In 2Chron ;3,1 , it is said: Solomon began to build the house of the Lord in Jerusalem, on Mount Moriah; there [the Lord] appeared to his father David, who had chosen the place belonging to him in the threshing floor of Ornan, the Jebusite. Jonathan Smith summarizes Jewish traditions and notes:

~ This is where the waters of the "Depth" were blocked on the first day.

~ It is the source of the first light of creation.

~ The site of the Temple was the first place there was, and is therefore the "center" of the world.

~ It was from there that the dust was taken to form Adam.

~ It is the place of Adam's first sacrifice.

~ This is the place of Adam's tomb.

~ It was there that Cain and Abel sacrificed, and therefore Abel was killed.

~ The Flood was caused by lifting the foundation stone of the Temple and releasing the waters of the Deep.

~ It was on the site of the Temple that Noah first sacrificed after the Flood.

~ It was on the premises of the Temple that Abraham was circumcised.

~ It was on the site of the Temple that the altar of Melchisedech stood.

---

[38] Josh , 24 , 26: Then Joshua wrote these things in the book of the divine law; He also took a large stone and set it up in that place, under the oak that was in the place dedicated to the Lord.

~ It was on this site that the altar for the sacrifice of Isaac was located.

~ It was on the site of the future Temple that Jacob had his vision of Bethel.

~ The Foundation Stone was the rock from which Moses made water flow.

~ Yahweh stood at the Temple site to stop the scourge

The Temple must embody peace, rest and sustainability. It is the service of G-d, one of the three enclosures, elements of the foundation of Jewish values, with the Torah in the Holy of Holies and charity which forms the link to the world.

To understand *the importance of the temple* , watch the interesting documentary: < tinyurl.com/importance-du-Temple >.

Flavius Joseph in *Judaic Antiquities* reports about the symbolism of the Temple of Jerusalem: "the three parts of the sanctuary correspond to the three cosmic regions (the courtyard represents the Sea - that is to say the lower regions - the Holy House representing the Earth and the Holy of Holies Heaven; the 12 slices which are on the table symbolize the 12 months of the year; the candelabra with 70 branches represents the Decans (that is to say the zodiacal division of the seven planets into tens) – the chariot of the soul, the Merkéva".
The Temple was not built on flat ground [39]but in successive stages on the side of Mount Moriah (for a

---

[39]< tinyurl.com/illustration-Temple >.

geological history of the construction of the Temple of Jerusalem, monograph of the Haram-ech-Chérif[40].

When Jerusalem became a Christian city, the very site of the Temple, ruined, was left as it was but, according to some (Anonymous of Plaisance, Cyril of Scythopolis, Gregory of Tours), a church, commemorating the presentation of Jesus at the Temple , was built by Justinian, between 531 and 543, on the edge of the esplanade, Sainte-Marie-la-Neuve; it will be destroyed by the Persians during the siege of Jerusalem in 614.

According to the Quran, the construction of the Temple was started by the prophet Daoud (David) and completed by his son, Souleymane (Solomon). Souleymane would have built it with the help of the jinns who were under his orders. It is in homage to his father that he finished the work.

The Temple of Jerusalem was alternately filled and abandoned by the inconstant crowd of Hebrews; a king of Egypt plundered it, a king of Israel finding that the example was worth following imitated it, another closed the doors and called other gods to other altars. Hezekiah restored his glory for a moment, but his son Manasseh broke the tabernacle of Jehovah. After four centuries of existence and varying fortunes, it collapsed in the fire lit by the Babylonian army. Rebuilt after the captivity, becoming both temple and fortress, it was completely overthrown on August 10, 71 AD by the army of Titus. On its ruins other sanctuaries were raised, in turn

---

[40]Melchior Vogüe, *The Temple of Jerusalem, monograph of the Haram-ech- Chérif , ...< tinyurl.com/monographie-Temple>.*

churches and mosques, depending on whether the fortunes of the East or that of the West dominate in Jerusalem [41].

The destruction of the temple heralds the messianic times . Basically, wasn't it an idol that was destroyed?

Today, all that remains of the Temple are the retaining walls of the esplanade built by Herod and the remains of the arches which allowed access to the esplanade. For Bob Cornuke, biblical explorer, the real location of the Temple would not be on the mountain (in fact the location of the Roman garrison) but down below, further south, in the city of David [42].

The distant *Al-Aqsa Mosque* is one of the main holy sites in Islam. Between 1969 and 1983, the dome of the *Al-Aqsa Mosque* was covered with aluminum by anodizing, which gave it a silver appearance. In 1983, for the sake of authenticity, it was given its original lead covering, dark gray in color .

In Venice, each synagogue is only a substitute for the destroyed Temple of Jerusalem. To remind us of this flaw, it includes a sign of imperfection such as a small defect in its black and white paving to remind it [43].

---

[41] Complete with this video documentary, *The Temple of Jerusalem through the generations* : < tinyurl.com/Temple-de-Jerusalem >.

[42] Video: <tinyurl.com/location-Temple>

[43] Video: <tinyurl.com/pavage-synagogue>.

Solomon's Temple

It is the first stone temple built in honor of the God of the Hebrews. Before the fourth year of Solomon's reign, the Hebrews celebrated the worship of YHVH as nomads, in a simple removable and transportable tent, in the Temple in the desert during the Exodus, then in Jerusalem while awaiting permanent construction. (to *Ælia Capitolina* as the Roman emperor Hadrian called it).

According to Thomas Römer, it was the Deuteromists who invented the construction reported in the Bible. In fact, according to the sources, he **considers that it would be a renovation which would have been installed in the temple of a solar divinity, an annex chapel for the tutelary god of the Hebrew kings.**

The temple acted as a focus of religious and cultural life, being the location of the sacrifices described in the Torah as *korbanot* . The supposed date of its completion would be around the 10th [century] BC. BC, that of its destruction by the Babylonians in -586 under Nebuchadnezzar.

The First Temple or Temple of Solomon was built, according to the Bible, by King Solomon in the 10th [century] BC. It is dated according to I Kings, 6, 1: "it was the 480th [year] after the children of Israel left Egypt, the 4th year of his reign over Israel, in the month of Ziv , which is the second month, that Solomon began to build the house of the Lord." Diodorus of Sicily, however, erroneously attributes its construction to Moses. "This colony was headed by the one called Moses, a man very remarkable for his wisdom and his courage. This Moses, having taken possession of the country, founded various cities there and - in particular - the one which is today the most famous and which is called Jerusalem. He also founded the temple which is the object of very great Veneration among them.[44]

Similarities with other temples in the region appear in the ornamentation and construction. Of Phoenician, Moabite and Syrian inspiration, built with the help of Tyre, this Temple attests to the syncretism and cosmopolitanism of King Solomon.

The true nature of the building is above all spiritual, art exists only to translate the idea; for the two civilizations, Israel and Egypt, we speak of the sacralization of art. Access to the Temple was reserved for the Cohens (the priests) [45]. A structuring of access authorizations to the space around the temple was very strict [46].

Through the Temple, Solomon wants to build a society open to transcendence. He wants to carry out a spiritual transformation of the world, lead it towards the path of perfectibility, transmute the human into the divine: the Temple must be the symbolic image of man and the world demonstrating that we must first live in spirit, carry out its reconstruction within itself in order to access the knowledge of the celestial temple. "Solomon's

---

[44]Book I of the Historical Library of Diodorus of Sicily: < tinyurl.com/Diodore-History >.

[45] Here is another representation of the structure of the enclosure delimiting the access zones: <tinyurl.com/zones-acces-Temple>.

[46]< tinyurl.com/espaces-acces-Temple >.

temple was not simply the binding of the holy book, it was the holy book itself. On each of its concentric enclosures the priests could read the word translated and manifested to the eyes, and they thus followed its transformations from sanctuary to sanctuary until they seized it in its last tabernacle in its most concrete form, which was still architecture the arch. Thus the word was enclosed within the building, but its image was on its envelope like the human figure on the coffin of a mummy [47].

The entrance to the building is to the east while the Ark of the Covenant is to the west (according to Ezekiel, Ez 42,4 : "The glory of the Lord entered the temple through the door which is turned towards the East." This orientation evokes the path which comes from the light, a path which passes through a law of interior becoming, through a spiritual transformation, the quest for personal integrity.

The Temple is the point of convergence between God and his creation, between the earthly Jerusalem and the heavenly Jerusalem.
The cabalists use the configuration of the Temple to inscribe what they call the four states of the universe through four states of sacralization. Starting from the squares we find:
The world of action: *Asiah* , the forecourt.
The world of forms: *Yetsira* , place of emotions; the vestibule or oulam (A).

---

[47] Victor Hugo, *Notre dame de Paris, Book V, This will kill that* , 1865: <gallica.bnf.fr/ark:/12148/bpt6k5674470n/f97.item>.

The world of ideas : *Briah* , place of intellectual thoughts; the palace or hekhal (B).

The world of spiritual emanation: *Atzilut* , place of feelings; debir, which has the same semantic root as dabar, the word in Hebrew (C). The darkness of the Holy of Holies should not be understood as the absence of light, but as its unmanifest principle, the invisible source at the origin of its manifested or visible aspect.

These worlds represent a route to follow, starting from the profane, visible, material, tangible world towards a sacred, subtle, hidden world which will gradually reveal itself to those who know how to get started.

In medieval religious works, depictions of church construction sites are titled "construction of Solomon's Temple".

The great Hagia Sophia in Istanbul, the Dome of the Rock in Jerusalem, the headquarters of the Knights Templar, and many medieval cathedrals were all designed as symbolic reaffirmations of the original.

The Temple of Zerubbabel

The second Temple, the Temple of Zerubbabel, was built upon the Jews' return from captivity in Babylon, around 536 BC. It was completed on March 12, 515. Following Cyrus' declaration calling on Israel to return and rebuild the House of G-d in Jerusalem, the first thing the Hebrews did was build the altar of stone, so that they can begin making offerings as quickly as possible.

The new altar was built 52 years after the destruction of the first temple, by Joshua and Zerubbabel in Jerusalem.

As Solomon had done, the builders hired the services of Sidonians and Tyrians to bring timber from Lebanon. "It was in the second year of their coming to the temple of God in Jerusalem, in the second month, that Zerubbabel the son of Shealtiel and Joshua the son of Yosadak, with the rest of their brethren, the priests, the Levites, and all the people who returned from captivity to Jerusalem, began the work, and they entrusted the Levites twenty years old and upward to supervise the work of the Temple of Yahweh" (Ezra 3:8). However, we find in II Chronicles 34.12 that it was King Josiah who rebuilt it and that the workers were under the supervision of Yahat and Obadyahu, Levites of the Merarite family; and Zechariah and Meshullam from the family of the Kohathites responsible for leading them.

The second Temple could not have the luster of the first. In addition, certain elements had been definitively destroyed or lost, and could not be replaced: the Ark of the Covenant, the Ourim and Thummim, the holy oil, the sacred fire, the tables of the Decalogue, the pot of manna, and Aaron's staff. It will be desecrated when, on the orders of Antiochos IV, an altar dedicated to Zeus is erected in the Temple and the Jews are forced to sacrifice pork to the Greek god. It will be reconsecrated with the episode of the oil which burns for 7 days and which will give rise to the feast of Hanukkah.

Herod's Temple

In the year 37 BCE, the Roman Senate handed over the crown of the Kingdom of Judea to Herod I the [Great], who removed political power from the priests. Herod's Temple of Jerusalem is the name given to the massive expansions of the Temple of Zerubbabel and the renovations of the Temple Mount, carried out by this paranoid and bloodthirsty king.

This project began around 19 BC. JC. The building was forty-five meters high and took more than forty-six years to construct (Jn 2:20). Flavius Josephus writes that when the sun shone on it, one could not stare at it for long because one was so dazzled by the whiteness of its stone and the gold of its decorations. The destruction of this temple by the Roman troops of Titus in 70 CE is recounted in *The Jewish War* by Flavius Josephus [48].

Ezekiel's temple

This is what I saw: an outer wall surrounded the Temple on all sides, and the man held in his hand a surveyor's rule six cubits long, taking the long cubit, a little larger than the ordinary cubit. He measured the thickness of the walls of this construction: it corresponded to the length of his ruler. He found the same dimension for the height. (Ezekiel ;40.5). The temple of Ezekiel's vision is that of the heavenly Jerusalem [49].

---

[48] The Temple during Herod's period, video: <tinyurl.com/Temple-sous-Herode>.

[49] Article, *The New Jerusalem is measured with a golden reed* : < tinyurl.com/measures-du-Temple >.

From the Temple to the Masonic Temple

In Freemasonry, the place where the outfits are held is called a temple. Like cathedrals and all temples worthy of the name, Masonic temples are oriented, at least symbolically: according to the east first, where the light comes from, then the south, where the sun shines, the north, the domain of the moon, finally the west, where the door is located that leads outside the sacred space. It is a semantic field of symbols where "while assuming an aesthetic dimension, the ornamental would have an epistemic vocation".

The various companionship societies which exist in France trace their origin to the construction of the Temple of Solomon; most of them adopted the myth of Hiram, although they gave themselves particular leaders. Some of the stonecutters are called children of Master Jacques, who was a sculptor and architect, colleague of Hiram, and to whom legend attributes a life and death quite similar to those of the latter. Father Soubise, also employed in the work of the temple, is the patron of the carpenters.

The Temple appeared for the first time in 1637 in Scotland, mentioned in the *Mason's Word* , in the Presbyterian Calvinist community.
The presence of the Temple of Solomon in Masonic legend is part of the unsolved enigmas. Of the 150 manuscript versions of the *Old Charges* , only two mention it, the *Regius* , 1390, and the *Cooke* shortly after.

Why after a total silence which lasted 300 years?

Was there cause and effect that, in 1665 in London, a Spanish Jewish rabbi, Jacob Jéhu de Léon, exhibited, at the request of King Charles II, a very pretty model of the Temple of Solomon [50]designed in Holland, which attracted enormous attention, an exhibition which continued with the same success until 1765, that is to say for a century? Or by the publication in 1688 of a work *The Temple of Solomon Spiritualized* by the Anabaptist writer John Bunyan, a well-known and renowned author?[51]

Desaguliers, as a good Anglican pastor, thought, perhaps, that the meetings of the FM should be held in a temple, to promote Newtonian deism because the construction of a new temple on an old one is a very common practice each time a "religion" takes over another. Thus the temples of the old deities are destroyed and those of the new ones are generally built on top, to bury the error and make the archaeologists happy. For example, this was repeatedly the case in the establishment of the Catholic religion: the Basilica of Saint Peter, in Rome, was built on an ancient temple of Zeus; the church of Saint Nizier in Lyon on a temple of Attis; the Holy Sepulcher in Jerusalem is built on a temple of Jupiter that the Romans had built on Golgotha and so on, the examples are very numerous and the reasons very simple. On the one hand we wanted to impose the new religion without leaving a trace of the place of veneration of the previous one and then we knew that the place was sacred and it always remained a sacred space.

---

[50]Image: <tinyurl.com/maquette-temple-Salomon>.

[51] John Bunyan, *The Temple of Solomon spiritualized* : <tinyurl.com/le-temple-spiritualise>.

But which temple to choose? Obviously it had to be a biblical temple, but which one to choose? The first temple of Solomon, that of Zerubbabel or that of Herod? The first, of course, the only one whose measurements are so well described in several books of the Holy Scriptures.

Perfect sketch of the universe for Willermoz, universal hieroglyph for Louis-Claude de Saint-Martin, **the Temple of Solomon is at the heart of lithocentric Freemasonry** . "The mathematical measurement of the building which is said to be the expression of the divine will executed by Solomon in relation to the plans given to Moses by God himself is the basis of all research into the fundamental laws of the universe. This direct relationship between matter and divine will could only be a source and a universal model for Newton. This universal model will be that of a rational spirituality rejecting trinitarianism in favor of deism, which will lead to the search for scientific and symbolic explanations, establishing the cross influence between man and great nature with a view to a new alliance". Also called the *Beth Hamikdach* , the house of sanctification, **the Temple of Solomon occupies a prominent place in the rites of Freemasonry as an allegorical, symbolic and spiritual backdrop.**

The Masonic Temple aims to be an image of the cosmos; from this point of view, the Temple of Solomon is the Solar Universe, and Hiram Abif, the Grand Master builder of the Temple, is the Sun who travels through the twelve signs of the zodiac, where he performs the mystical drama of Masonic legend .

It is not sacred in itself, but it becomes sacred through the direction given to thought. Freemasons come to perfect themselves by working on themselves, taking its construction as a model.

For the RER: D- What does the Lodge represent? A- The Temple of Solomon mystically rebuilt by the Freemasons.
Built in the image of man and in the image of the universe, to study the symbols of the temple is to study both (Willermoz). An analysis of the symbols of the Masonic "temple" is given by Rebold in *Histoire Générale De La Freemaçonnerie* of 1850 [52].

For the REAA, the Masonic Temple, like the Lodge of Cathedral Builders, is not the Temple itself in which God is supposed to come and reside according to the description given in the Book of Kings, it is under construction in the West and can be confused with the city.

In rituals, through distortion, the word temple is used in the same way, whereas it should only refer to the temples of biblical and Masonic mythology (Temple of Solomon, of Herod, of Zerubbabel, of Enoch , etc.) The correct term is "lodge" when the lodge is ritually opened, "lodge premises" or "lodge room" when it designates the building (*lodge room*). In Scotland and Ireland, we also use "chapel" (*chapel*) and, very often, this is one…Even if the decor of the Masonic temple evokes in certain aspects the Temple of Solomon, the work does not begin

---

[52] Rebold, *General History of Freemasonry* : <tinyurl.com/Histoire-Franc-masonry>.

or end in the temple, but in the lodge. The space in which the rituals are represented is therefore no more the Temple than the cathedral or the synagogue. Its appearance is only a paradigm supporting the myth, a theater setting changing with the degrees of work, "a complete and autonomous system of thought, within its own limits."

The temple, as a permanent premises dedicated to Masonic work, is the subject of a specific consecration ceremony.

CSR/RE. The premises, as such, distinctly from the lodge (human group), are the subject of a specific consecration ceremony, the same for the apron of the Most Venerable and his collar (both being transmitted from successor to successor), as well as for the lodge Bible and, possibly, for the sword and the banner.

For there to be a work of architecture, there must be design. To create the Masonic temple, it is generally sufficient for 7 regularly initiated masons to meet under the starry vault (the building would therefore be, rather, a hypethrum), trace the box table on the ground, materialize the columns, the sun, the moon, the square, the compass. It is not even necessary that the volume of the sacred law be there, it is enough for those present to mentalize it, for them to place themselves at the office posts and open the work so that the temple exists and becomes this sacred place which will disappear when the work is closed. In Freemasonry, it is understood that the temple does not pre-exist: it is the masons who build it both collectively (humanitarian temple) and individually (human personality, cubic stone called philosophical in hermeticism).

The Masonic temple, the lodge, is the place of a symbolic representation of the world. Some rituals ask the question of its dimensions to which it is answered: its length goes from west to east, its width from north to south, its height from nadir to zenith. The Sepher Yetsirah gives the same description of the cosmic space ruled by the 7 planets associated with the double letters (authiot): "Seven doubles. High and low, East and West, North and South. The six ends: above and below, front and back, right and left correspond to the six days of creation.

Three axes are thus defined: east/west (east-west), the axis of light, that of the direction of the work and the questions and answers between the Venerable and his supervisors; noon/north, (north-south), axis perpendicular and complementary to the first, it sees the members of the lodge distributed around each of the columns; nadir/zenith (high-low), axis of the infinitely small and the infinitely large, of the earth and the sky, the material and the immaterial. The infinity of this space indicates to the Freemason that it is built everywhere.

Let us add to this the dimension of time and the dimension of spirituality. The true dimension of the temple to be built is that of the man to be built.

As Oswald Wirth wrote: let us know how to transform ourselves into a temple and protect ourselves from all profanation so that the Mysteries which are accomplished in us are those of true royal art ! It is the contemplative power which builds the Temple, and the

Temple, erected in the imaginal, thus becomes the real Gate of Heaven [53].

The Masonic temple is rebuilt each time the works are opened and demolished each time they close. The outfit is the place and time of a construction site. This construction can only be achieved when the elements of space, time and quality of the participants are respected and verified, through rituals in the form of questions and answers: the covered lodge, the age of the members according to the degree of 'opening. The Freemasons are the presence of the living temple of which the buildings are only the symbols. In this living, anthropomorphized temple, which has its image in each of the Freemasons, the true Mysteries are accomplished, in other words those of life. The symbolism of the Masonic temple is an incentive to develop our own project, our own architecture, remembering however that the time of the project, that of reflection and design, is a necessary prerequisite to that of the construction site, which is the time of action and achievement.

Can rituals alone create this sacred space? This architecture, immaterial by nature, remains to be built, or rather to be rebuilt with each Outfit, both outside the temple and inside oneself [54].

---

[53] Durand, *The thoughts of Henry Corbin and the Masonic temple* : <tinyurl.com/Corbin-et-le-temple-maconnique>.
[54] François Gruson, *Masonic architecture, architecture of the spirit* : <academia.edu/5183992>.

The picturesque History of Freemasonry and ancient and modern secret societies by F.-TB-Clavel will take you around the world, in 1844, to visit some remarkable Masonic temples [55], notably in Altenburg, Baltimore, Brunswick, Brussels, Cape of Good Hope, Darmstadt, Edinburgh, Frankfurt am Main, Freiberg, Gloeau, Gotha Halle, Leipzig, London, Marseille, New York, Nordhausen, Paris, Philadelphia, Port-Au-Prince, Posen, Rotterdam.

A contemporary visit updates the look at some of these Masonic temples in No. 5 of the digital Masonic Review *La Plume et la Pensée*[56]

Number **6** of the Revue *La Plume et la Pensée* devoted to " *Places of Remembrance, between memory and history* " evokes in particular *the headquarters of the GODF* by Dominique Goussot; *the GLD* F Headquarters by Christophe Bitaud; *the seats of the DH* by Francois Mercier and *the Temple of Tours* by Christophe Bitaud [57].

---

[55] *The Picturesque History of Freemasonry and Ancient and Modern Secret Societies* by F.-T. B.-Clavel <tinyurl.com/temples-remarquables>.

[56] *The pen and the thought n°5* : <tinyurl.com/la-plume-et-la-pensee>.

[57] *The pen and the thought n° 6* : <tinyurl.com/monuments-pour-FM>.

...

6 HIRAM, KING OF TYRE, A LITTLE-KNOWN CHARACTER

Hiram king of Tire is the son of king Abchal, contemporary and ally of David and Solomon.

Freemasonry remembers from the King of Tire the triangulation that he composed with King Solomon and Master Hiram, in particular by the supply of cedar wood from Lebanon which was used in the construction of the Temple of Jerusalem.

And also Hiram, king of Tyre, sent his servants to Solomon, when he heard that he had been crowned king in place of his father; for, from all times, Hiram had been a friend of David (IKings 5, 15). And now give orders to cut down the cedars of Lebanon; my workers will help yours, whose wages I will pay you according to what you tell me. For, you know, there is no one among us who is skilled in cutting down trees like the Sidonians, (IKings 5, 20) The fleet of Hiram, which had brought gold from Ophira, also brought sandalwood, in great abundance, and precious stones. And of this sandalwood the king made railings for the house of YHWH and for the royal house, and harps, and lyres for the singers. There never came so much sandalwood, nor has it been seen like this until this day (1 Kings 10,11-12).

Numerous texts of rabbinic tradition grant this king a privileged place little mentioned by Freemasons.

Hiram of Tire (the Talmud has a legend that Hiram was granted 600 years of Paradise as a reward for the Cedars of Lebanon which he provided for the construction of Solomon's Temple) is among the ten righteous who "entered the garden alive of Eden: Enoch son of Jared, Eliezer the servant of Abraham, Bithiah the daughter of Pharaoh, Sera ḥ the daughter of Asher , the prophet Elijah, the Messiah son of David, Ḥ iram king of Tyre, Eved the Ethiopian , the king's servant, Javetz b. Rabbi, and Yehoshua b. Levi . "[58]

Josephus, in his treatise against Apion informs us on the testimony of Menander, that King Hiram rebuilt the temple of Melkart [the god Ba'al of Tyre]. If Herodotus is correct in his data, then he must have existed for more than seventeen centuries. Hiram is said to have, then, abandoned old Tire and taken up residence on the adjacent island, surrounding the town square with high hewn stone walls. Hence the temple, which Herodotus would have seen, would have been that of Hiram.

The book *Yalkutt* (which is a compilation of the Midrash) says that Hiram built for himself, in the middle of the sea, a paradise of seven heavens (like Babel), and that to punish him for his great pride, Yod sent Nebuchadnezzar against him who allegedly destroyed his

---

[58]Jean-Yves Legouas The messiah in biblical *and rabbinical literature* : <tinyurl.com/le-messie-dans-litterature>.

paradise and demolished it into pieces when he was about 600 years old [59].

Rav Touitou David recounts the life of this king and also reports the tragic end of Hiram after his defeat against Nebuchadnezzar [60].

Eight kilometers east of the city of Tire is the Tomb of King Hiram of Tire [61]. It is an imposing mausoleum and one of the most interesting monuments in the Holy Land. It is notable less for its beauty and ornament than for its grandeur and durability. Crowning a graceful hill, it consists of a pedestal and a sarcophagus. The first is composed of four layers of immense blocks of limestone, about ten feet high; the latter is cut from a solid block and measures twelve feet long, eight wide and six high and is surmounted by a pyramidal cover five feet thick. The ends of the lid are beveled, the top rounded and it is fitted so carefully that it is difficult to remove. On the north side of the monument is an arched vault 20 feet square and 12 deep, which undoubtedly served as the place for the final rest of the royal family.

---

[59] John Yarker, *The Arcane schools* : <tinyurl.com/The-Arcane-Schools>.

[60] Video of Rav David Touitou: <tinyurl.com/Hiram-roi-orgueilleux>.

[61] Tomb engraving of King Hiram of Tire: <tinyurl.com/tombeau-Hiram-de-Tyr>.

A few words about the famous cedars of Lebanon[62]

Cedars are above all "sacred" trees. The narrator linked them inseparably with many of the most grandiose events in biblical history. *These are the "trees of the Lord", the "cedars of Lebanon which he planted"* (Ps. civ., 16.) . *Here is the rest of this forest, the wood of which was taken for the Temple of God in Jerusalem;* (IRois ;5 and 6).
They express greatness, strength, power and glory. But in denouncing the judgments of the Lord on the proud and arrogant, the prophet declares: " *For the day of the Lord of hosts will be on all who are proud and high, and on all who are high, and it will be brought low; against all the slender and majestic cedars of Lebanon and the oaks of Bashan* " (Isa, 2.12-13). As an illustration of Jehovah's displeasure with royal pride, He asks Ezekiel to speak thus to the king of Egypt, and to his throng: " *Behold, there was in Lebanon a superb cedar, with beautiful branches, with shady foliage , tall in stature; its top pierced the clouds ...*" (Ezekiel ; 31,3 -14) Breaking the cedars and shaking the enormous mass on which they grow, are figures chosen by the psalmist to express the terrible majesty and the infinite power of God. " *The voice of the Lord is powerful; the voice of the Lord is full of majesty. The voice of the Lord breaks the cedars; yes, the Lord breaks the cedars of Lebanon".* (Ps ;29 ;4,5).

The forests of the East, always near the point of ignition under the intense rays of a vertical sun, are frequently set on fire by the carelessness of those who have taken refuge in their recesses, and the devouring element continues its ravages until until vast plantations are

---

[62]Engraving, John P. Newman, *From Dan to Beersheba* , Chap. XIV, 1892: <tinyurl.com/cedres-du-Liban>.

consumed . To such a conflagration the prophet Zechariah compares the destructive operations of the Roman armies under Vespasian and Titus against the Jews, when the nobles and rulers were slain, the city and temple reduced to ashes, the people put to the sword , be sold into slavery, and the whole country devastated. "Open your doors, O Lebanon! Let the fire wreak its havoc among your cedars! Lament, cypress, for the cedar is fallen, the proud giants are cut down! »

In the second part of the *Dumfries Manuscript* it is written: "What is the mystery of cedar wood? Cedar, cypress and olive wood are not subject to putrefaction and cannot be devoured by worms; thus the human nature of Christ was not affected by putrefaction and corruption .[63]

Adoption Freemasonry, centered on Noah, evokes the analogy between the incorruptibility of cedar wood and the true virtuous mason [64].

---

[63] p.14/16 : <tinyurl.com/Dumfries-manuscript>.
[64] P.54: <tinyurl.com/vraie-maonnerie-d-adoption>.

7 THE WORKERS OF THE TEMPLE, WHAT FREEMASONRY LEARNS FROM THEM

According to the Texts (I Kings, 5, 13 to 18), the workers of the Temple of Solomon employed in the construction of the Temple were approximately 183,300, namely: 30,000 corvee men sent alternately to Lebanon and to the construction site, 70,000 burden porters, 80,000 stone cutters in the mountain and 3,300 masters (*harodim*), but according to II Chronicles 2:18 , the masters were 3,600, but according to Kings 9:23 they were 550.

The *Old Charges* also mention the number of workers. Thus the *Cooke Manuscript* [65] would indicate that there were 80,000 masons at work while the *Lansdowne Manuscript* [66] indicates 24,000 *Workers of Stone*. Few manuscripts of the *Old Charges* , in their historical part, indicate the exact number.

---

[65] *Score thousand masons at his work* : <tinyurl.com/CookeManuscript>.
[66] P.72/105: <tinyurl.com/Manuscript-Lansdowne>.

This is what *Anderson's Constitutions report* : "3,600 princes or master masons to conduct the work according to the instructions of Solomon, with 80,000 stonecutters or companions in the mountain; and 70,000 laborers : in all 153,600 in addition to the levy, under Adoniram, to work in the mountains of Lebanon alternately with the Sidonians, namely 30,000, making in all 183,600". It is added in a note of the *Constitutions* of 1723 (p.4): "In Kings (I, v. 16), they are called *Harodim* (hé, resh, daleth, iod, mem), Governors or Provosts assisting King Solomon and who were put to Work. Their number is only 3,300; but in the Chronicles (II, v. I8), they are called **Menatzchim** (men, noun, teth, eth, iod, men), Watchers and Comforters of the People at Work, and they number 3,600. It is possible that 300 of them could have been more curious Artists and Supervisors of the other 3,300; or again, that they were not so excellent, but only Deputy Masters for replacements in the event of Death or Absence: thus, there were always 3,300 active Masters in total. Or again, they could be the Supervisors of the 70,000, **Ish Sabbal** (aleph,iod,schin, samek,beth,lamed), men of Pain or Workers, who were not Masons but served the 80,000, **Ish Chotzeb** (aleph, iod, schin eth, tsadé, beth), men of Carving, also called **Ghiblim** (guimel, beth, lamed, iod, men), Stonemasons and Sculptors, or even **Bonaï** (beth, noun, iod), Stone Builders. They belonged partly to Solomon and partly to Hiram, King of Tyre. (Kings, I, v. 18) ."

The Giblim , their name comes from *Ghiblim* גְּבָלִים used in the Bible (IKing 5, 32), with the meaning of mason : " the Ghiblim (Gibléans) squared and shaped the wood and stone for the construction of the temple " . *Giblos* or *Gibeah* is a mountain near Jerusalem where, according to legend, the stone necessary for the construction of the Temple was extracted.

The Giblites inhabited the city and region of Gebal, in Phoenicia, near Mount Lebanon, they were under the domination of the king of Tyre.

It is with the form "Ghiblim" that Pastor Anderson spells it in his Book of Constitutions of 1738 where we read [translated from English]: it is said that in 1350 Jean de Spoulce, called Master of the Ghiblim, rebuilt the Saint-Georges chapel. This word and its context of use seem to come from the *Geneva Bible* (1560) which mentions them in a margin note to the Bible verse 1 Kings;5,18 . We can read this verse which gives according to the translations: "The workers of Solomon and those of Hiram, the Giblians or Gebal or specialists from the city of Byblos or even the workers of Solomon and those of Hiram and the Giblites): the Hebrew word is Giblim גְּבָלִים , who are said to be excellent masons ; they are generally journeymen , sometimes apprentices, never masters .

Calcott, in his 1769 book, *A candid disquisition of the principles and practices of the Society of free and accepted masons* , further cites 300 **harodim** , governors or masters, 3300 **menatzchim** , Canaanite overseers, and 70,000 who were the survivors of the ancient Canaanites, considered as burden-bearers. [67]

---

[67] Wellins Calcott *A candid disquisition of the principles and practices of the ... Society of free and accepted masons:* < tinyurl.com/ouvriers-du-Temple >.

We find in *The Perfect Mason or the True Secrets of the Four Grades of Companion Apprentices, Ordinary Masters and Scots of Freemasonry* of 1744: "When it was a question of rebuilding the temple of the Lord, Zerubbabel chose from the three states of the masonry the most capable workers; but as the Israelites had many obstacles and obstacles to suffer during the course of their work, from the Samaritans and other neighboring nations, the work would never have been brought to its end, if this prince had not would have had the precaution of creating a fourth grade of masons, whose number he fixed at 753, chosen from among the most excellent artists. These not only had inspection over all the others, but they were also responsible for ensuring the safety of the workers; They made the rounds every night, both to advance the work and to recognize pitfalls or prevent attacks from their enemies. Their job being much more difficult than that of other masons, they were also granted more advantageous pay; and to be able to recognize them, Zerubbabel gave them a special sign and words."

In the *Ritual of the Marquis de Gages* from 1763 [68]a clarification of what could have been the master's touch of gratitude to get paid during the construction of the temple, before Hiram's death specifies that "The *word which was changed by death that these unfortunate Companions gave to our Master Hiram was "Jehovah", pass **3593, number of the Masters** who had the direction of the works* ". After Hiram's death, a meaning was given to these four numbers, it is said that: three form, five compose, nine were sent to search for the body of the Master and three murdered him.

---

[68] < tinyurl.com/Rituels-MarquisDeGages >.

The rituals of the York Rite also evoke the texts of the Old Testament: "For its construction, three great masters were employed, assisted by three thousand three hundred masters or supervisors of the work, eighty thousand companions or stone cutters who worked in quarries and mountains, and seventy thousand apprentices or burden bearers," to which the Bible adds 30,000 corvée men.

The Regulator of the Grand Lodge of 1801[69] thus gives the count of the workers: the count which was made of all the workers brings them to 183,300. History calls them **proselytes** , which in our language means admitted foreigners, that is to say initiated. Know: 5000 men intended to cut cedars in Lebanon, who served in thirds for a month; 70,000 apprentices, 80,000 journeymen and 3,300 masters. The inhabitants of Mont-Cibel shaped cedars and cut stones.

The 13th degree of the REAA (Knight of Royal Arche), indicates that There were 3568 Masters, who had been active during the construction of the Temple.

Note that Solomonic cement was composed of wheat flour, milk, wine and oil. This singular composition teaches that the Architect used gentleness, kindness, wisdom and power to cement the world. It also teaches that the stones are only held together by the work (wages) of the workers.

Masonic texts present Salomon as the client, the project manager and the architect.

---

[69] *The Regulator of the Grand Lodge of 1801:*
<tinyurl.com/Regulateur-GL>.

Architects enjoyed great consideration in the eyes of philosophers such as Plato or Aristotle; they surpassed the painters and sculptors who were only simple imitators of reality.

In architecture, everything was geometry and numbers and like all sciences of the time, the whole thing was intimately mixed with philosophy. For example, when an architect invented a stage setting for a play by Aeschylus taking perspective into account, the innovation attracted the attention of the philosophers Anaxagoras and Anaximander who then scientifically defined the problems of perspective. The portrait that Vitruvius draws, and that all authors in the 15th and 16th centuries take up at leisure ' is ^{that} of a universal man, naturally knowing the laws of geometry, mathematics, the use of materials of construction and the art of foundations, but also versed in optics, meteorology, music, medicine and astronomy, and possessing sufficient knowledge of philosophy, history and jurisprudence…

According to a legend, reported in particular in the third writing of codex IX of Nag Hammadi, Solomon *happened to call on demons* , in particular, to be able to complete the construction of the Temple. This codex was thus deciphered: "King D[av]id, who established[s] the foundation(s) of [Je]rusalem, and [his][son] Sal[o]m[o]n, [whom he begat in[a] adultery (and) who built Jerusalem [thanks] to the Demons, because he had received [a power] black. However, when he had finished building, he locked the demons in the temple (and) he put them in seven jars. [They remained] for a long time in the jars, abandoned there. When the Romans were brought to Jerusalem, they removed the lid from the jars and at that time the Demons came out of the jars. res] … [However, since those days, (the Demons) [remain] with the men who are [in] ignorance and [and they have remained on] the earth".

8 THE MYSTERY OF THE SHAMIR

John Yarker, in an article on *The York Rite and Ancient Masonry in General* , notes that "in truth, workers illegally plotted to extort from Hiram Abif a secret, that of the amazing animal which had the power to cut the stones. The secret that was lost by the three Great Masters is that of the shermah insect (shamir), which was used to give a perfect polish to stones ." Considering this remark by Yarker, would the operating secret of the shamir be "what has been lost"?

Similarly, in the presentation of the *Wooler Ritual* , which resembles Yarker's text, we read in a third degree catechism: "After the construction of the Temple, the workers of the highest degree, known as " *Most Excellent* " , accepted the great secrets concerning the noble In... Sh..., which was what constituted the secret of the three Grand Masters and [for] which HAB was killed"; the use of abbreviations proving the formerly esoteric nature, or supposed to be so, of the information.
In his *Miscellanea Latomorum* , Dr. William Wynn Westcott offers a passage from an old ritual which speaks specifically of the secret of the shamir insect and the three Great Masters. This Masonic tradition is ignored today

The shamir, from the Aramaic *chamira* , "like a flint", was a supernatural organism.

Was shamir a mineral, a plant or an animal?

In an Abyssinian legend it is supposed to have been a kind of wood or grass.

In biblical Hebrew, the word shamir (שָׁמִיר) was used in two senses: either a point made of a very hard substance like diamond (Jeremiah 17.1 ; Zechariah 7.12), or sharp thorns (Isaiah 5, 6).

The Talmud and later great rabbis described how the shamir, passing along the surface of a stone , can split it perfectly into two pieces. The Talmud states that it was the "gaze" of a living creature that caused wood or stone to break . According to Rabbi Ba'hya, the shamir was used by Bezaléel at the time of the construction of the Tabernacle in order to engrave the names of the tribes on the precious stones embedded in the pectoral of the High Priest. Moses' staff, possibly made of shamir, could have split this rock in two to make water flow. Its supernatural essence came from the fact that it was said to have been created at dusk, on the eve of the first Shabbat , during the Six Days of Creation [70].

This miraculous shamir would have been specially created at the beginning of the world for this operative use. According to this legend, when Solomon asked the rabbis how to build the Temple without using iron tools,

---

[70] In the sixth chapter of the fifth book of Pirkeh Avot – the book of the fathers – it is written: Ten things were created on the eve of Shabbat at dusk: the mouth of the earth, the mouth of the well, the mouth of the donkey, the rainbow, the manna, the rod (of Moses), the shamir, the writing, the engraver (point), and the tablets (of the Law)

to comply, of course, with the injunction of Deuteronomy (Exodus ; 20,21 : If, however, you erect for me an altar of stones, do not build it with hewn stones; for, by touching them with iron, you have made them profane), they drew his attention to the shamir with which Moses had engraved the Name of the tribes on the breastplate of the high priest [71].

In the Jewish Encyclopedia, in the tales and legends of Israel [72], we find this legend which tells that, on the recommendation of the rabbis and in order not to use iron, Solomon cut stones using the shamir, an animal, a worm whose mere touch split the stone. This legend is also found in Arabic literature and even in the Koran.

In Talmudic literature there are numerous references to *Shamir*. Unusual qualities have been attributed to him. For example, he could disintegrate anything, even as hard as stones. Among his possessions, Solomon considered it the most wonderful. King Solomon was eager to possess the Shamir because he had heard about it. Knowledge of the Shamir is in fact attributed by rabbinical sources to Moses. After much searching for Shamir the size of a grain of barley, he was found in a distant land, at the bottom of a well, transmitted to Solomon, but strangely, he lost his abilities and became inactive for several centuries later, around the time Solomon's Temple was destroyed by Nebuchadnezzar.

---

[71]To understand the importance of the pectoral of the High Priest of the Hebrews through the symbolism of the gems embedded there, read article no. 2 of 1892, *Urim and Thumim* : <tinyurl.com/L-Initiation-nvembre-1892-2 >.

[72]Arthur Weil, *Salomon and Asmodee* : <tinyurl.com/Salomon-et-Asmodee>.

Surprising and curious *Shamir* ? What is it?

It is assumed that the legend is based on a corruption of the word *Smiris* , Greek for emery, which was used by ancient engravers in their works and medallions, and that the name Shamir is simply the Hebrew forma of the Greek word [73].

According to medieval authors, Rashi, Maimonides and others, *Shamir* was **a creature alive** , a worm; arguing that Shamir could not be a mineral because it was active. This magical worm was endowed with the power to modify stone , iron and diamond, by its simple gaze. Furthermore, rabbinical sources have transmitted the description of the engraving of the names of the twelve tribes on the twelve precious stones of the high priest's breastplate (the pectoral); Moses did this not by carving, but by writing with a certain fluid and "showing" them to Shamir, or exposing them to his action. In the opinion of modern authors, the expression "shown to Shamir" clearly indicates that it was the gaze of a living being that carried out the division of wood and stones. It is admitted, however, that in Talmudic sources and Midrashic literature, it is never explicitly stated that the Shamir was a living creature. So Shamir/schamir/samur, as we find the expression, a worm the size of a grain, or something else, a stone according to the different literary sources ?[74]

---

[73]Mackey, *Encyclopedia of Freemasonry* , p. 709.: <tinyurl.com/shamir-grec>.

[74] *The Shamir and the stone worm* : <tinyurl.com/shamir-et-pierre>.

An old source, *The Legend of Suleiman and Testament of Solomon* work written in Greek, probably early in the third century CE, refers to Shamir as **a green stone** , the shamir being a green crystal stone of great power[75] Only one shamir is known to have existed. It is carved in the shape of **a beetle** , a scarab of the species *Sacer ateuchus* . This is the reason why the shamir was confused with an insect.

But how could a greenish stone cut the hardest of diamonds with just its gaze?

Let's take a look at what Louis Guinzberg recounts, in 1909, in *The Legends of the Jews* , who, inspired by rabbinical exegesis, relates the story in a very fantastic way: the shamir was created at dusk on the sixth day with other extraordinary things. It was no larger than a grain of barley and possessed the remarkable power of cutting the hardest diamonds. It is for this reason that it would have been used by Bezaléel (בְּצַלְאֵל), and not Moses, at the time of the construction of the Tabernacle to engrave the stones of the breastplate worn by the high priest [76]. First the names of the twelve tribes were traced in ink on the stones which were to be set in the breastplate, then the shamir was led over the traced lines and they were thus engraved. A miraculous circumstance, the route did not carry any particle of stone .

---

[75] According to the chronicles of Tabari Med Ibn Djarir, by Sabine Baring-Gould, Ahimaaz bin Tsadok, Louis Ginzberg, John D. Seymour, Chap.7, page 10 note 31: <tinyurl.com/legende-Soliman>.

[76] < tinyurl.com/pectoral-grand-pretre >.

The shamir was also used to cut the stones from which the Temple was built , because the law forbade the use of iron utensils for any work intended for the Temple. To preserve it, the shamir should not be placed in any iron or metal receptacle, as this would cause it to burst. It is kept wrapped in a wool blanket which in turn is placed in a lead basket filled with barley bran. The shamir was kept in Paradise until the day Solomon needed him. He sent the eagle to search for the worm.

The manner in which Shamir was kept safe may give us a clue: "The Shamir cannot be placed in an iron vessel for safekeeping, nor in any metal vessel: such a vessel would burst. It is kept wrapped in wool inside a lead box filled with barley bran. This phrase is taken from chapter 48b of the Babylonian Talmud and contains an important clue; because, with current knowledge we can easily guess who or rather what Shamir was: it was a radioactive substance; radium salts, for example, acting on certain other chemical substances, can emit a yellow-green luminescence.

This would explain how the high priest's pectoral had been engraved : the letters were written in ink, and the stones were exposed one after the other to the "gaze" or radiance of the Shamir. This ink must have contained powdered lead or lead oxides. The parts of the stones which were not protected by lead disintegrated without leaving particles of dust which, according to this Talmud, appeared particularly marvelous. The parts protected by lead ink stood out in relief on the surface of the precious stones (most gems, such as diamond, sapphire, emerald or topaz, are discolored by radioactivity. Others Precious stones , such as opal, are made of hydrated silica crystals.

Alpha radiation disintegrates them by breaking the bond with water; it volatilizes without leaving any residue).

Solomon's most valuable possession, his *Shamir,* did not survive over time, it became inactive. The usual version of the story, "the missing Shamir", does not correspond to the exact translation of the Hebrew text. The word *batel* used to describe Shamir's end, or disappearance, has only one meaning: "To become inactive. "

In the four hundred years between the construction of the first Temple and its destruction by Nebuchadnezzar in 587 BC, a radioactive substance could have become inactive (radium loses about one percent of its radioactivity every 25 years).

Could Hiram's secret be that of the use of a sort of radioactive laser that the evil companions wanted to take from him?

To complete this aspect read the text *Modern physics and the chamir* :[77]

---

[77]Lamed.fr, *Modern physics and chamir:* <tinyurl.com/physique-et-chamir >.

9 NOTIONS OF ARCHITECTURE

Public space is a place of memory and bearer of economic, historical or spiritual meanings which go beyond and embrace the entire territory of the city. An emerging creation in one neighborhood can have a resonance on the rest of the city. The monuments show that the city is not only made of stones or concrete but also of a history of men who, through their activity and their creativity, have forged its identity. As Victor Hugo writes, " during the first six thousand years of the world, from the most immemorial pagoda of Hindustan to the cathedral of Cologne, architecture was the great writing of humankind. And this is so true that not only every religious symbol, but also every human thought has its page in this immense book and its monument.

From being strictly religious, Greek architecture took on a whole new dimension, and the Hellenistic cities gradually developed civil architecture in stone. The principles of symmetry and rationalism are still there, but a new concern appears: harmonizing architecture with the configuration of places and landscapes. The theaters, built into the hillside, are perfect examples. Everywhere, sports buildings or private stone residences appear while stoas delimit the urban setting. Each building now benefits from the same care as religious architecture before, and demonstrates a taste for pageantry and splendor.

There are privileged places, connected to the sacred interior and collective, which allow one to rise towards a better understanding of oneself and others as well as of the Indefinable. Sacred places like cathedrals, as well as ancient temples, and more particularly the Temple of Solomon, are built according to human proportions. The plan of Chartres highlights this: at the crossing of the transept is the heart, the head being in the sanctuary or Holy of Holies. The project manager works in the material he must animate and his rhythmic proportions respond to a living mathematics, plant or human.

The theological conception of art in the 13th century can be summed up as a search for perfect mediation between the pure beauty which belongs only to God and the mirror which the artisan-artist must offer to Him through his work so that it reveals itself to the eyes of men. In such a spiritual context, where the World is seen as the work of the greatest architect, there is no real separation between spirit and matter, art and technology. According to Jacques Trescases, "A true architecture must allow a meeting of stone and light in a relationship which is not that of accusatory lighting but with a desire for assumption of one towards the other. In this touching of the divine and of human creation, in this flow of light from balcony to column, from column to sculpture, light becomes a metaphysics and a partner at least equal to man. Charles-Edouard Jeanneret, known as Le Corbusier, also defined architecture as "the correct and magnificent play of volumes under light", by light he meant Knowledge [78].

For architectural considerations of the constructions of the Ark and the Tabernacle, as well as the Temple and the Palaces of Solomon, see the text by Daniel Ramée devoted to Judea in his *General History of Architecture... Volume 1.*[79]

Architecture is a science of rhythms that sacralizes space. Light is always used in the design of places of worship. Whether religious or atheist, designers seem to have no choice but to manipulate light. The use of light in religious buildings seems to have been established since Vitruvius. [80]Its contribution goes beyond the simple fact of utility, it becomes a material "giving" life to the images of the divinities. Necessary to express anagogical beauty, it promotes through its influence the idea of the divine by sublimating the atmospheres of places of meditation. We can also think that the relations of the dimensions of the constructions are numbers whose vibrations induce particular states in beings, allowing spiritual energies to enter the body.
stone books , revealing the Great Work illustrated, among other things, by an alchemical bestiary.

According to Vitruvius, the architect, in addition to mastering the art of building, must be versed in

---

[78]<academia.edu/5184076/>.
[79]Daniel Ramée devoted to Judea in his *General History of Architecture... Volume 1:* <tinyurl.com/etude-architecture>.
[80] Abdelouahab Bouchareb, *Vitruvius: temples and light* : <tinyurl.com/temple-et-lumiere>.

disciplines as diverse as letters, geometry, optics, arithmetic, history, philosophy, music, medicine, law and astronomy, so many fields which undoubtedly founded the Italian conception of the architect as a universal man. From the Middle Ages to the Renaissance, building is not a pure technical activity but an art that mobilizes the highest human knowledge. Geometry, this extraordinary science which finds its summit in stereotomy, in some way materializes the Mason's ability to grasp the complexity of the world [81].

The books of Anderson's Constitutions, begun by Anderson, continued by Entick and Noorthouck, contain, under the title of history of Freemasonry, in reality a history of the progress of architecture from the earliest ages. In the ancient manuscript of Anderson's Constitutions, the science of geometry as well as architecture are in fact identical to Freemasonry. For Roger Dachez, "architecture is the elective place for the expression of religious and spiritual thought and philosophy from around the world."

Victor Hugo ends the chapter *This will kill that* in *Notre Dame de Paris of 1482* with the apology of the book of paper against the book of stone : "Every day a new foundation rises. Independently of the original and individual contribution of each writer, there are collective contingents...there too there is confusion of languages, incessant activity, tireless work, fierce competition from

---

[81] Another look at the operative origins by José Gulino, in *The Rule and the Compass or some operative sources of the Masonic tradition* , 2013.

all of humanity, refuge promised to intelligence against a new flood, against a submergence of barbarians. It is the second Tower of Babel of the human race.[82]

Architects enjoyed great consideration in the eyes of philosophers such as Plato or Aristotle; they surpassed the painters and sculptors who were only simple imitators of reality.

In architecture, everything was geometry and numbers and like all sciences of the time, the whole thing was intimately mixed with philosophy. For example, when an architect invented a stage setting for a play by Aeschylus taking perspective into account, the innovation attracted the attention of the philosophers Anaxagoras and Anaximander who then scientifically defined the problems of perspective. The portrait that Vitruvius draws, and which all authors in the 15th and 16th centuries take up at leisure, is that of a universal man, naturally knowing the laws of geometry, mathematics , the use of construction materials and the art of the foundations, but also versed in optics, meteorology, music, medicine and astronomy, and possessing sufficient knowledge of philosophy, history and jurisprudence....

The medieval architect uses as emblems of his dignity the three instruments of geometry: the compass, the ruler and the square. It is therefore above all to theoretical knowledge and conceptual abilities that it refers and not simply to the profession practiced. Yet the architects of

---

[82]Victor Hugo, *This will kill that* in *Notre Dame de Paris* p. 142: <tinyurl.com/ceci-tuera-cela>.

Gothic cathedrals have remained silent. For what? Answers in Laurent Ridel's text on the anonymity of cathedral architects [83].

In architecture, one of the problems is the basic measurement reference.

Here is an attractive hypothesis: **with the drop of water, we will be able to measure everything!**
The Nile flood lasted 4 months, bringing silt to the crops. To find the measurements of the fields after the recession, the harpedonapts used knotted ropes. The problem with the unit of measurement for their spacing was that they had to find a fixed referent (the parts of the pharaoh's body, feet, cubits, etc. changed with each new reign); an attractive hypothesis holds that the diameter of a drop of water from the Nile was retained, its dimension on an impermeable surface is claimed to be constant and measures one centimeter ; they will name this unit "royal finger" (10 royal fingers will be called the royal hand, the decimeter, 100 royal fingers equal one royal leg, one meter).

In addition, from the sixth of the circumference of the royal leg, the measurement of 52.36 (cm) drops of water will become the royal constant (royal cubit, also called the Hebrew cubit). All of Egypt will thus have as a standard, a universal constant called the royal cubit, a few drops of water! This is how they integrated for the measurements of the pyramids, the universal constants

---

[83]Laurent Ridel, *Decoding churches and castles. Why do the names of their architects remain unknown?* < tinyurl.com/architectes-inconnus >.

that they were the first to discover, Pi (which would be 22, the letters of the Hebrew alphabet, divided by 7), Phi, the royal cubit and the royal leg as, among others, in the royal chamber of Khufu [84].

It is not so much the measure of the unit that counts but the relationships between the elements of the construction which will produce the forms [85]. " You should know that the essential part of the geometric system of the first Renaissance is a modular system, in which each order of architecture defines an arithmetic proportional rule between the widths, heights and depths of a building and its parts. This modular system, already widely described by Vitruvius, makes it possible to adjust an entire building from a whole number of modules whose basic unit is determined by the diameter of the column [86].

Masonic Architecture

A relevant analysis was made by François Gruson in his thesis *Ritual practice and form of space: the Masonic temple: form, type and meaning* [87]. We will retain some thoughts from this.

---

[84]For **medieval measurements** refer to the article by Alexis Seyd: <irna.fr/Mesures-medievales.html>.

[85]Video, Fehmi Krasniqi, *The Great Pyramid K2019* : < tinyurl.com/Grande-pyramide>.

[86] François Gruson: *The spirit and the symbol in architecture, the divine proportion* : <tinyurl.com/la-divine-proportion>.

[87]François Gruson, *Ritual practice and form of space: the Masonic temple: form, type and meaning* : <tinyurl.com/rituel-et-espace>.

Architecture built by Freemasons for Freemasons (i.e. the architecture of Masonic temples) is Masonic to the extent that it implements a functional program (mainly linked to the practice of ritual and feasts) and symbolic (by the establishment of the space and decorations) linked to a specifically Masonic practice.

The study of ancient rituals or iconography as it appears from the origins in the disclosures allows the reconstruction of a true history of Masonic places, from taverns (pubs in London, back rooms of caterers in Paris), salons of notables in the provinces, then premises designed for this purpose, and finally premises strictly dedicated to Masonic uses, finally called "temples" after the Revolution. The Masonic temple most often constitutes a setting, like a theater set, on which symbolic interpretation can take all its power.

For François Gruson, Masonic architecture is a kind of vehicle which allows us to move from the material and tangible world, that of the body and immanence, to the world immaterial , that of the spirit and transcendence. The creation in the 18th century of the Masonic temple as an architectural model responds to a double need, both mental and physical. On the mental level, the development of a codified system of spatial and ornamental devices fixes the roles of the different actors at the same time as it fixes the ritual practices of Freemasonry (proxemics). On a physical level, this model responds to a need to perpetuate these devices and facilitate their material implementation, including in its most practical aspects.

On the frontispiece of the 1786 edition of Anderson's Constitutions, the engraver Cipriani represents the temple of the Grand Lodge of London, (built in 1775-1776 to the plans of the architect Sandby), loaded with symbolic scientific tools and a nebulous allegorical apparition of theological virtues (*The Truth, holding its mirror, illuminates the interior of Freemasons' Hall*).

However, it should be noted that a distinction clearly appears between a visible, even shown, architecture, which is that of an institutional Freemasonry linked to the religious or political practices of the country (mainly Anglo-Saxon countries) or of the time, and an invisible architect, either because she has disappeared, or because she can seem hidden in that she is not supposed to be seen by the lay public.

The large temple on rue Jules Breton in Paris, headquarters of the International Mixed Masonic Order Le Droit Humain, listed in the inventory of Historic Monuments in June 2013 "takes on an activist dimension aimed at displaying, in public space, the nature and convictions of the Order and, through the evocation of the original myths, it proclaims, to other obediences, the legitimacy of the presence of women in Freemasonry.

The form of Masonic architectural space is to be understood as the result of a ritualized practice of space.

Some notable Masonic temples

Extract from *the Picturesque History of Freemasonry and Ancient and Modern Secret Societies* by F.-TB-Clavel (1844)[88]

ALTENBURG (Upper Saxony): Location of the Archimedes lodge, with three boards, one of the most beautiful in Germany. A medal was struck on the occasion of its inauguration. **BALTIMORE** (United STATES): Masonic Temple for the assemblies of all the lodges of this city. This building cost the company 40,000 dollars (212,000 francs). **BRUNSWICK** : Local of the Charles lodge with the crowned column. **BRUSSELS** : Temple of the Lodge of Philanthropic Friends, one of the most beautiful, largest and most complete known. It is particularly intended to confer the different grades of the ancient and accepted Scottish Rite, to which the lodge belongs. **CAP DE BONNE HOPE** : The Dutch lodge, Good Hope, established in this locality, had a magnificent temple built in 1805, the expense of which amounted to more than a ton of gold. **DARMSTADT** : Temple of the lodge of Saint John the Evangelist, at Concorde, built in 1817. The Grand Duke of Hesse donated the land, all the necessary timber, and a considerable sum, taken from his cassette and from STATE funds , intended to cover other construction costs. The Grand Duke himself laid the first stone of the building, at the head of the brothers, on June 14. This is the first example of a public procession of Freemasons in this part of Germany. **EDINBURGH** : Local of the Grand Lodge of Saint-Jean, in Niddry-Street. This building was formerly a hall intended for giving concerts, and which was called the Sainte Cécile hall. The Grand

---

[88]F.-TB- Clavel, *Picturesque history of Freemasonry and ancient and modern secret societies* : <tinyurl.com/Clavel-Histoire-pictoresque>.

Lodge acquired it and had it appropriated for Masonic work. The lodges within his jurisdiction helped him greatly with their subscriptions. The lodge of the Chapelle de Marie alone paid a sum of 1000 pounds sterling (25,000fr.). - The lodge of Mary's Chapel also owns the room where it holds its sessions, in High Street, Edinburgh. **FRANKFURT AM MAIN :** Each of the lodges in this city has had premises built at its own expense for its sessions. Most of these premises cost considerable sums. Special rooms are dedicated to circles, frequented every evening by members of the lodge and by masons from other workshops in the city, who visit each other. There are libraries, reading rooms, and even restaurants. **FREIBERG** (Saxony): Temple of the Three Mountains Lodge. **GLOEAU** (Lower Silesia): Temple of the lodge at Loyal Meeting. **GOTHA :** Temple of the Ernest au Compas lodge. Very elegant and pretty construction . **HALLE** (Magdeburg region). Temple of the Lodge of the Three Swords. **LEIPZIG :** Buildings of the Freemasons' Sunday School. **LONDON :** Freemasons'hall. This magnificent building, whose construction cost the English masonry more than 750,000 francs, was erected in 1775. The length of the building is 92 feet, its width 45, and its height more than 60. The decoration of the The meeting room is incredibly rich. The vault is decorated with a sun in burnished gold, surrounded by the twelve signs of the zodiac. The organ, which is placed in the eastern part, cost 25,000 francs. Only the Grand Lodge meets in this room. Many of the lodges in London, counties and overseas possessions have also had large buildings constructed at their own expense for the holding of their assemblies. **MARSEILLE:** Most of the lodges in this city own the premises in which they hold their sessions. The temple of the lodge of the Scots is one of the largest and most richly decorated known. The lodge itself is eighty to one hundred feet deep. **NEW YORK :** Freemasons'hall. The first stone of this beautiful monument was laid on June 25, 1826. The building is in the pure Gothic style built in granite stones. The frontage is 50 feet; depth of 125 feet; the height of 70 feet, not counting the turrets which have more than 10. Among the singularities presented by this construction, we must mention the middle door, which is of solid oak, in a single piece and 4 feet high. thickness. **NORDHAUSEN** (Thuringia): Temple of the Lodge of Crowned Innocence. It is a very recently constructed building. **PARIS : Masonic** Temple , rue de la Douane. This temple, intended for the sessions of the Grand Orient of France and the lodges within its jurisdiction established in the capital, has nothing remarkable on the outside; but the interior is vast, suitably distributed and decorated with as much taste as wealth. The other premises in Paris are operated by entrepreneurs who rent them to the lodges per session. **PHILADELPHIA** (United States): Masonic temple in the Gothic style of architecture. This building was erected by subscription, and cost enormous sums. It is the most beautiful monument in Philadelphia. The Grand Lodge and all the lodges of the jurisdiction established in the city and surrounding areas, the chapters of Royale-Arche, and the encampments of Knights of the Temple and Knights of Malta, hold their assemblies there in turn. It was built in 1819 on the site of another Masonic Hall which had been destroyed by fire. The commissioners responsible for collecting the subscriptions presented themselves at the house of the famous Stéphen Gérard, so well known for his immense fortune. He registered for 500 dollars (2,675 francs). Surprised that a man who had long since stopped frequenting the lodges nevertheless made such a magnificent donation, the collectors expressed their thanks in the name of masonry. "So I subscribed for a very large sum !" said Stéphen Gérard. He took the list again, and added a zero to the number he had written there; which brought his subscription to 5,000 dollars, or 26,750 francs. He immediately paid the amount into the hands of the commissioners, telling them: "This is more worthy of Stéphen Gérard, and will justify your thanks a little better." In many other cities in the United States, lodges have had beautiful and vast Masonic premises built, at their own expense. But, either on whim or because the construction of these premises lacks the necessary amenities, the brothers generally prefer to assemble on the highest floor of some private house. **PORT-AU-PRINCE** : Temple of the Star of Haiti, the first stone of which was solemnly laid on January 25, 1842, by the grand master of the Grand Orient of Haiti, General Inginac, and by a large influx of masons decorated with their insignia. **POSEN:** Masonic Temple, built in 1817, for the lodge assemblies of this city. The first stone was laid, with a large Masonic device, on May 5, by all the brothers gathered. **ROTTERDAM** : Union Lodge Temple, built in 1805.

10 ORDERS OF ARCHITECTURE

On the cartouche unveiled during the augmentation ceremony, during the second journey of the becoming companion, we can read "The Arts", sometimes "The orders of architecture".

Architectural order is given by the proportions and arrangements given to the parts of a building so as to form a whole, not only regular, but above all harmonious. In the 16th ^{century} , suggested by Vitruvius, Sebastiano Serlio in his *Regole generali architectura* established on a board the canons of Western architecture with a representation of five orders which will become the classics until today. These five modes of arranging architectural elements were used in Antiquity: the Doric order, the Tuscan order, the Ionic order, the Corinthian order and the composite order.

An order consists of **three main parts; the pedestal, the column and the entablature** . Each of these parts is subdivided into three others which are also called architectural members. Thus the pedestal has a base, a die and a cornice; the column has a base, a shaft and a capital; the entablature an architrave, a frieze and a cornice. It sometimes happens that the first of the three main parts (the pedestal or even the base of the column) is removed without the rest ceasing to constitute an order; but when the entablature is removed, or when it is modified to the point of depriving it of one of its three constituent parts, all of the remaining members can no longer receive the name of order.

As for the column, whatever deletions of members have been made to an order, it is never missing, because it is the essential, indispensable part, and without which there would be no architectonic order. . Also it is by the size of its shaft that we regulate the proportions of the various orders, and by the shape and decoration of its capital that we characterize them best. The fundamental principle of orders is therefore the module, that is to say the basic width, taken from the diameter of the column. The whole system is then broken down according to a purely proportional scheme. Their geometric relationships are extremely complex.
Of the five orders retained by classical architecture, two, the Tuscan and the Doric, have their capitals composed solely of moldings while the other three have their capitals decorated with foliage or scrolls called volutes.

The Greeks used Doric, Ionic and Corinthian, to which the Romans added Tuscan and Composite. According to Vitruvius, if the Doric column symbolizes the body of the man, the Ionic that of the woman, the Corinthian order symbolizes the body of the young girl. The reference to a plant also makes it possible to make it the symbol of nature and, more generally, of life and its renewal. The proportional system determines morphological characteristics close to those of the human body. Thus, the Doric order, considered stockier due to its proportions, is equated with virile strength. Conversely, the Ionic column, more slender, is recognized as undeniably feminine, also because of its capital decorated with scrolls. This sexualization of orders of architecture is important in the question of the meaning that we want to give to the building that uses them. Without making it a general rule, we will use the Doric order for the temple dedicated to Apollo at Delphi, the Ionic order for the temple of the victorious Athena in Athens, and the Corinthian order for the temple of Vesta in Rome (We will appreciate the complexity of the architectural orders with *The ten books of architecture of Vitruvius, corrected and newly translated into French with notes and figures* , 1673, in particular Book IV of the work which evokes the origin and the invention of the three main orders [89].

A curious article, *The Great Mystery of the Freemasons Discovered* , published in 1724, reports the contents of a document found on a dead Freemason, where we find questions and answers from what appears to be a Masonic instruction booklet in which The orders of architecture and the geometric shapes are related : the Tuscan, the Doric, the Ionic, the Corinthian and the

---

[89] *The ten architectural books of Vitruvius, corrected and newly translated into French with notes and figures,* starting on page 99: <tinyurl.com/les-ordres-principaux>.
Lovers of architectural order will read with interest the review on the subject written by Philibert De l'Orme in 1585 in his work *Architecture* , in the *Cinquiesme Livre* chapter: <tinyurl.com/ordre-architectural>.
See also The *Rules of the Five Orders of Architecture* by Giacomo Barrozzio De Vignole:
< tinyurl.com/architectural-rules >.

Composite correspond to the Base, the Perpendicular, the Diameter, the Circumference and the Square [90].

"One might wonder about the non-traditional Masonic custom of assimilating the three pillars of the lodge to three columns of different orders. If we can understand the assimilation of Strength with Doric virility and Beauty with the feminine elegance of the Corinthian, we understand less the rapprochement of Wisdom with the Ionic. This reminds us, if we needed it, to what extent the interpretation of symbolic language reflects above all the concerns of the time which formulated them [91].

William Preston in his work *Illustrations of Masonry* , specifies the particular classes of the Architectural Order and explains the qualifications required for advancement in each [92].

The Composite Order

The composite order is an architectural order of Roman creation whose appearance, by combination of Ionic and Corinthian capitals, is specially determined by a capital with scrolls and acanthus leaves. The composite column has a height equal to ten diameters.

---

[90] To download to read *The Great Mystery of the Freemasons Discovered* : <tinyurl.com/textes-a-telecharger>.

[91] Note 15 by François Gruson of the text: <academia.edu/5184244>.

[92] William Preston, *Illustrations of masonry:* <tinyurl.com/illustrations-FM>.
To understand the difference between Romanesque style and Gothic style, Laurent Ridel, *Roman vs Gothic* , video: <tinyurl.com/roman-vs-gothique >.

Wiliam Preston says: Composite is made up of the other orders and was invented by the Romans. Its capital has two rows of Corinthian leaves, and Ionic volutes. Its column is quarter round like the Tuscan and Doric orders, is ten diameters high, and its cornice has simple dentils or modilli.

This pillar is usually found in buildings where strength, elegance and beauty are united.

The Corinthian Order

It would be due to the sculptor Callimachus of Corinth. Corinthian art appeared in the 4th [century] BC. J.C. Just like the Ionic order, it focuses on representing decorative motifs. Nature offers models to sculptors. Thus, to adorn the capital, the artists imitated an ornamental plant with elegantly cut leaves, called acanthus, and it is this plant decoration, described as virginal, which defines the Corinthian order. The Corinthian order is the second of the three Greek architectural orders. According to Vitruvius, if the Doric column symbolizes the body of the man, the Ionic that of the woman, the Corinthian order symbolizes the body of the young girl. Vitruvius explains its origin in the first chapter of Book IV of his *Ten books on architecture* : [93]"A young girl from Corinth, having died, her nurse placed a basket on her tomb containing her familiar objects. To protect its contents, she placed a tile on top. The basket having been placed on an acanthus root , the leaves and stems soon enveloped it and constrained by the tile, curved, thus forming volutes . The Athenian sculptor Callimachus

---

[93]Vitruvius, *Ten books of architecture:* <tinyurl.com/ordre-corinthien>.

passing by this tomb, seduced by this unexpected arrangement of the leaves around the basket, decided to imitate it and adapt it to the columns he was creating by adjusting the proportions and style of the model to this model. 'Corinthian order'.

Wiliam Preston says of it: The Corinthian, the richest of the five orders, is considered a masterpiece of art and was invented in Corinth by Callimachus. Its column is ten diameters high, and its capital is decorated with two rows of leaves and eight volutes which support the abacus. The frieze is decorated with curious devices, the cornice with dentils and modillions. This order is used in majestic and superb structures:

The Doric Order

Its name comes from Dorus, son of Hellên, king of Achaia and the Peloponnese. Doric art, the oldest, flourished in the 5th century. av. Twenty grooves bring relief to the massive columns which end at the top with capitals with flat spines, smooth, without sculpture, bare, without decoration. The Doric style is characterized by the absence of a base.

Vitruvius explains that it is built on the basis of the proportions of the human male body: "Whatever the size of a column at its foot was, they [the architects] gave it a sixfold height, including the capital. This is how the Doric column took the imprint of the proportions, the strength and the beauty of the human body [94].

---

[94] Ibid: <tinyurl.com/ordre-dorique>.

The Doric order is the simplest, most stripped-down of the three Greek orders. Wiliam Preston says: The Doric order, simple and natural, is the oldest and was invented by the Greeks. Its column is eight diameters high and rarely has any ornaments on the base or capital, except for moldings; although the frieze is distinguished by triglyphs and metopes, and the triglyphs make up the ornaments of the frieze. The solid composition of this order gives it preference, in structures where strength and noble simplicity are primarily required. The Doric is the best proportioned of all the orders. The various parts of which it is composed are based on the natural position of solid bodies. In his first invention, it was simpler than in its current state. Later, when it began to be decorated, it took the name Doric; for when it was built in its primitive and simple form, it was given the name Tuscany. Therefore, Tuscan precedes Doric in rank, because of its resemblance to this pillar in its primitive state.

The Ionic Order

It would come from the Ionians of Asia and the temple of Ephesus.
The Ionic order developed in the second half of the 5th century BC. AD It is characterized by the addition, at the top of the fluted columns which have become more refined, of a sculpted motif. A volute winds like a spiral at the top of the column shaft. The Ionic order (also called Ionic column) is revealed in particular by its scrolled capital, by its shaft decorated with 24 grooves, and by its molded base. In the volutes would be evoked the wave of the goddess of beauty, Venus, the lady of the sea because born of the sea, which refers to Aphrodite,

Astarte or Asherah. Vitruvius recounts that the Ephesians, on the occasion of the construction of the temple to Artemis (Diana), a female divinity, wanted to create an order whose proportions would be those of the woman's body, more slender, i.e. a height eight times equal to the diameter of the column [95].

Wiliam Preston says of it: The Ionic bears a sort of middle proportion between the most solid and the most delicate orders. Its column is nine diameters high; its capital is decorated with scrolls and its cornice with dentils. There is both delicacy and ingenuity in this pillar; the invention of which is attributed to the Ionians, as was the famous temple of Diana in Ephesus. It is said to have been formed after the model of a pleasant, elegantly shaped, coiffed young woman; in contrast to the Doric order, which was formed after that of a strong and robust man.

The Tuscan Order

The Tuscan order, order of classical architecture, is a simplified form of the Greek Doric architectural order. Tuscan columns are seven diameters in height, including the base and shaft. The spine is more rounded and the barrel more curved. Vignole assigns the following proportions to the Tuscan order: entablature, 3 modules and 6 minutes or 3 ½ modules, including 1 module 4 minutes for the cornice, 1 module 2 minutes for the frieze and 1 module for the architrave ; columns, 14 modules, including 12 for the shaft, 1 for the base and 1 for the capital; pedestal, 4 8-minute modules, including 3 8-minute modules for the die, 6 minutes for the base and

---

[95] Ibid: <tinyurl.com/ordre-ionique>.

6 for the cornice; decrease from base to top, 6 minutes; intercolumn, 4 modules 8 minutes. What especially characterizes the Tuscan order is the absence of any ornament.

Wiliam Preston says: The Tuscan is the simplest and strongest of the five orders. It was invented in Tuscany, where it gets its name. Its column is seven diameters high; and its capital, its base and its entablature have few moldings. The simplicity of construction of this column makes it eligible where solidity is the main object, and where ornament would be superfluous.

It is only through historians that we know of the existence of this order because no specimen of ancient Tuscan construction has survived except to compare it to the Palladian order [96].

Is it a style considered too "Stuartist" that the Hanoverians of the so-called Anderson Constitution did not retain it among the styles of architecture?

---

[96]Wikipedia: <tinyurl.com/ordre-palladian>.

11 THE OBELISK, A MONUMENT FOR WHAT SIZE?

The meaning of obelisks

Roasting spit is what the word *obéliskos* **means in Greek , which gave rise to obelisk** . The origin of the name tells us the shape: a stake to pass through the animal to be roasted. Our obelisk has straightened itself and what it crosses is the sky, space, it is an arrow pointed in the direction of the immutable center of light: the sun; **he himself becomes a ray of sunshine.** The obelisk will be intimate with what the sun **can do** . The sun gives time, the one who divides the day, the one who repeats the seasons.

The sun looks at the earth and measures it. Let's question him.

Say sun, what time is it?

The obelisk will be **gnomon** , a giant sundial needle whose cast shadow indicates time; and the higher it is, the more precise the calculations are.

At the time of Edfu, between Karnak and Aswan, built on the order of Ptolemy III and his son, there is a famous pylon, the 6th which played the role of gnomon.

The Emperor Augustus had one built in Rome, on the Field of Mars, in the year 10 BCE. The dial consisted of an obelisk approximately 22 meters high, brought from Heliopolis. The obelisk is still in Rome, but in Montecitorio Square. It cast a shadow on a semi-circle traced on a marble paving on the ground. It did not have a graduation and the time was only indicated by the position of the end of the shadow, identified using time lines. This type of sundial has a disadvantage: the end of the shadow becomes blurry in dim light. To remedy this, the Romans placed a sphere at the top of the obelisk, which cast a clearer shadow. Already for Anaximander (pre-Socratic) the tip of the gnomon is the image of the earth floating in the universe, like the cathedrals will be the overturned hulls of the land-ship sliding through the heavens.

Say sun, what date is it?
The obelisk will of course be **a meridian**
The image of the Sun is projected each day on the meridian line at the time of true solar noon. Every day, this image changes place on the meridian line and thus marks the date. The extreme positions are reached at the solstices. A meridian is thus a natural calendar.
In Paris, two historic meridians exist: One, drawn according to the calculations of Gio Domenico Cassini by his son Jacques, is located at the observatory. The other, started by the watchmaker Henri Sully and completed in 1743 by the astronomer Charles Le Monnier, is located in the Saint Sulpice church. It is a copper strip 40 meters long embedded in the marble: it starts from the South transept and continues to an obelisk placed against the North transept which receives spots of light indicating the equinoxes. The copper line

established in 1727 represents the course of the sun's ray which enters the church through a hole located in the south window of the crossing. The ray ends its course at its northern end on the obelisk, where vertical markers are drawn. Depending on the height reached by the sun's ray on the obelisk, we were able to determine the spring equinox, Easter Sunday and the time of noon. This set is what we call a chaise longue.

Say sun, give us the measure of the earth
In Greek, this word gnomon designates that which understands, decides, judges, interprets and distinguishes, a rule which allows understanding. The construction of the sundial depicts the shadow and natural light intercepted by this rule, a knowledge device.
It was with the help of an obelisk (in this case the lighthouse of Alexandria built around 300 BC) that Eratosthenes (he was appointed head of the library of Alexandria), around 205 BCE, calculates the first estimate of the earth's circumference. The method used by Eratosthenes is described by Cleomedes in his *Circular Theory of the Celestial Bodies* .

Using the difference in inclination of the Sun's shadows on the day of the summer solstice. Eratosthenes knows that in Syene, today Aswan in Egypt, on the day of the summer solstice, at noon, the sun's rays fall vertically to the ground because they illuminate a well to its bottom. At the same time in Alexandria, a city located approximately on the same meridian but further north, the Sun is not at the zenith. The obelisk of this city casts a very measurable shadow towards the North. With the vertical of the place (the height of the lighthouse), the length of the shadow of the obelisk makes it possible to know the angle made by the direction of the Sun and thereby to determine that made by the two cities from the center of the earth. To deduce the value of a meridian (circumference passing through the poles), it "is enough" for Eratosthenes to estimate the distance separating the two cities. According to the myth, a bematist [97] then counted 5000 stadia. The calculation of proportionality with an angle of 7.2 degrees (the angle at the center equal to that calculated on the surface according to the property of alternating-alternating angles) and a measurement of 157.5 meters for 1 *stadium* gives 39375 km (the circle having 360° the calculation is established as follows: 5000x157.5/7.2x360) to compare with the 40007.8 currently measured!

Thus the gnomon, giving this passage from light to dark, says that he knows. This idea is in these words of Michel Serres: "Yes, geometry is precisely named after its mother the earth on which what falls from the sky is measured. Marked with the help of the gnomon, it remains in the shadow like a foundation, like a foundation dug under science; geometry slumbered under the earth or dreamed in the radiance of the sun. The gnomon of the ancient Greeks or Babylonians gradually awakened it along the singular forms common to shadow and light. This is what Thales did by developing the foundations of geometry in the 6th

---

[97] A bematist (from ancient Greek βηματιστής) is an ancient Greek surveyor who measured the distance between two points by counting the number of steps (in Greek βῆμα / bêma); here in this case those of a camel whose steps were reputed to be equal and regular.

century BC , he did it notably in the shadow of the pyramid of Khufu. Having established a relationship between the size of his own height and his shadow cast under the Egyptian sun, and having measured the length of the pyramid's shadow, he transposed this same ratio to calculate the measurement of the pyramid's height. This ratio which allows one to go from small to large, in the similarity of proportions, is called a homothety ratio. Perhaps it was a stick stuck in the sand which served as a measure? Maybe it was Khafre or Mykerinos, whatever. We are, like Thales, in the shadow of all the pyramids which, in a relationship of homothety, from the shadow of a stick or from ourselves standing in all the lights, allow us to calculate the immensity, to bring it back to our dimension or conversely to give us the measure of the greater than us. We are geometers because we entered here.

The obelisk will be the intimate symbolic representation of the sky and its immensity.

By its **verticality** , the obelisk is similar to the vast family of standing stones, it becomes the link between heaven and earth, the mediator between here below and infinity, between the finitude of life and the eternity of death. This is why the obelisk will be erected, as a link with the cosmic forces, at the entrance to temples and tombs .

For the Egyptians, the top of the obelisk, called the pyramidion, is often covered in gold because it is the cosmic mountain, the primordial hill, the first land emerged from the waters on which the first ray of the sun landed. An analogous idea is attributed to Hermes Trismegistus for whom the pyramidal summit symbolizes the *demiurgic word, the first ungenerated power but emerged from the father and governing all created things.* This is why obelisks could be made of precious materials : Tuthmosis III (c. 1504 – c. 1450 BC) had two obelisks built in solid electrum (metal containing 75% gold), measuring 6 .50 m high and weighing 32 tonnes each.

The shape of the pyramidion obliges us to say a few words about the symbolism of the triangle when it is *in some way an imaginary representation of the metamorphoses of all aspects of the origin* . For Pythagoras The triangle signifies the triple nature of the first differentiated substance or the consubstantiality of the manifested Spirit, of matter, and of the Universe their son. This consubstantiality emanates from the point, the true esoteric Logos, this is what Hermes Trismegistus also says.

This triune monad is an equilateral triangle. The vertex is the ONE; not the number but the unity which is in contact with the void, the Aïn-sof of Hebrew gnosis, the Mystery of Mysteries (in those times zero had not yet been invented). The unit contains the 2 which is the first number because there must be the 2 for there to be either increase or division, for there to be something else and it is this **something another** which allows us to say that the 2 founds the 1 which then differentiates itself from the uncountable unit. **With the 2, the 1 separates from the unit.** *It is in the manifestation of the beginning that the One becomes the number one.*

Augustus will exploit these symbols as part of his personal propaganda. Indeed, as Valbelle recalls: "From the reign of Augustus, the transport and erection in Rome of a Heliopolitan obelisk dedicated to the sun god associate these monuments characteristic of the Egyptian solar religion with a solar theology integrated into the 'imperial ideology'.

His successors did not fail to do the same. Caracalla made Isis a deity of the Roman state. Nero, an admirer of oriental despotism, showed a keen interest in Egyptian symbols and particularly in obelisks. Aurelian even adopted the solar god as supreme god of the Empire. Finally, Constantine also had obelisks moved from Egypt to Rome. Adorning squares, temples, circuses, funerary buildings, the obelisk became an essential ornamental element of ancient Rome.

The monumental obelisk becomes a sculpted report and will naturally take place to celebrate significant events of a reign.

Since the dawn of time, figurative representations of the King in the capital, palaces and castles have functioned as a staging of the monarchy.

Signs of power which indicate where **authority resides** , these signs participate in political representation and its avatars.

As an architectural form, the pyramid is already a vestige. Before fulfilling any function whatsoever , before bearing witness to what took place where it stands, it offers itself as the monument of itself: memory of memory or monument dedicated to memory. The pyramid inscribes the place in the place, recalls the place to its memory of place. Hence the favor it enjoys among architects placed before the commission of an urban signal.

Cathala in 1790 thus planned a Bastille square with a column which "would represent the most interesting events of the reign of Louis XVI and the Revolution.

" The bas-reliefs speak of the storming of the Bastille, the arrival of the king and queen in Paris, the oath of His Majesty on the Constitution and the adherence of the provinces to the decrees of the Assembly. On July 13 of the same year, Barère requested that an obelisk be decreed built with the stones of the Bastille, where human rights, the storming of the Bastille and the Federation would be engraved. A deputation of artists came to the podium in September 1791 to propose that a column be built on the Field of the Federation, where the conquests of Liberty would be engraved, while Mangin and Corbet suggested starting without further delay a monument dedicated to the events of the Revolution, "figured under symbolic features."

The obelisk of Port Said, erected in memory of the city's martyrs, still stands in the middle of a large square. It is planted on an immense base 6 meters high decorated with bas-reliefs representing the different phases of the popular struggle against imperialism: Revolution of July 23, 1952, nationalization of the former Suez Canal Company. A verse from the Koran is engraved on the base.

Under the Directory (government of France from 1795 to 1799), relations deteriorated between the United States and France. From 1798 to 1800, there was a maritime war between the two great republics with seizures of merchant ships on both sides. As soon as power was entrusted to him (December 1799), Bonaparte, who was an admirer of the United States - he had a bust of George Washington in his office - worked to restore peace and friendship between the two nations. He invited President John A dams to begin peace negotiations.

Consequently, Olivier Ellsworth, William Davie and William Vans-Murray arrived in Paris on April 2, 1800. Bonaparte was able to bring to the negotiations all his common sense, his spirit of justice and his desire for peace and thus arrive at an agreement which received the title of the "Convention of Mortefontaine" signed on September 30, 1800. Two days later, on October 2, 1800, the First Consul gave a big party in Mortefontaine to commemorate it.

A flamboyant obelisk, whose pedestal was decorated with allegories celebrating the union of the American and French Republics, illuminated its surroundings.

As an art invested with an expressive purpose, the obelisk in France wants to mark the absolute power of its monarchs , it wants to mark its extent.

However, the cult of King Louis It is because this cult is turned as a priority

1 – towards posterity (hence the importance of the obelisk which symbolizes eternal fame),

2 – towards the upper classes (it is very rare to find a statue of the king in a village of this nation of peasants),

3 – towards foreign courts.

Hunger, cold, epidemics, war to boot: this is the origin of the great peasant revolts of those called the Croquants, the Nu-Pieds, the Lustucrus, this is the origin of the discontent which rumbles not only among Protestants, but also among those close to the king. They found themselves in 1793 in front of the pyramidal obelisk of Vaise, to destroy it because this obelisk necessarily affirmed everything that has just been said about obelisks.

It is said that the Freemason builds himself like a temple (of Solomon) or like a cathedral.

But, remembering these verses taken from Victor Hugo 's *Recueils d'Automne* : **Alas! More grandeur contains more nothingness / The bomb rather reaches the giant obelisk / Than the turret of doves** , I wonder if it would not be more humble if it were only built as a hive?[98]

---

[98] See the first chapter *Hive, bee, honey.*

ABOUT THE AUTHOR

Jacques-André editor
TU, Letters of Passion, 2001 (Laure de Noves Prize)

EDITIONS of La Hutte
To light the way, A philosophical approach to Freemasonry , 2011
Vocabulary of the Apprentice Freemason , 2nd edition *, 2012*
Vocabulary of the Freemason Companion , 2012
Master Freemason Vocabulary , 2013
Drawing elements with ruler and compass, The Masonic Concordance , 2015
What does it mean to cut your stone ?, 2015

EDITIONS ledifice.net
Gathering what is scattered , 2020
Vocabulary of the Apprentice Freemason , 3rd edition *, 2020*
Vocabulary of the Freemason Companion , 2nd edition *, 2021*

Ubik EDITIONS
Once upon a time, Hiram , 2021
Masonic gestures , 2021

Numérilivre EDITIONS _
Masonic traces, the spirit of geometry , 2022

Dervy EDITIONS
Vagabond Dictionary of Masonic Thought , 2017 (**literary prize of the Masonic Institute of France** *, Essays and Symbolism category)*
Freemason. How to move from profane to sacred , 2023

www.ingramcontent.com/pod-product-compliance
Lightning Source LLC
Chambersburg PA
CBHW012305240726
48656CB00008B/2560